THE JEWISH FOUNDATION OF ISLAM

BY

CHARLES CUTLER TORREY

PROFESSOR OF SEMITIC LANGUAGES
IN YALE UNIVERSITY

Introduction by
FRANZ ROSENTHAL

KTAV PUBLISHING HOUSE, INC.
NEW YORK

By arrangement with Hebrew Union College — Jewish Institute of Religion.

Originally published as the Hilda Stich Stroock Lectures at the Jewish Institute of Religion. First Published 1933.

MS: Koran
Islam -- Relations -- Judaism
Judaism -- Relations -- Islam

Dedicated

to my dear friend

DR. GEORGE ALEXANDER KOHUT

Library of Congress Catalog Card Number 67-18817

Manufactured in the United States of America

INTRODUCTION

Charles Cutler Torrey (1863-1956) was born in Vermont and educated at Bowdoin College and Andover Theological Seminary. Following the custom of the times, he went to Germany in order to obtain the higher scholarly training which was then not available in this country. The famous authority whom he wisely chose as his mentor was Theodor Nöldeke (1836-1930), the greatest Semitist of his own time and, perhaps, of all times. In 1892, Torrey completed his formal education with the publication of a doctoral dissertation written in Strasbourg under Nöldeke's direction. The small pamphlet of fifty-one pages, which appeared under the renowned imprint of E. J. Brill in Leiden, indicated its contents by its title: *The Comercial-Theological Terms in the Koran.* Its principal conclusion was that the commercial terminology of the Qur'ân was characteristically Arabic and that it consisted almost entirely of native words, not acquired from other languages, in contrast to other terms of Arabic theology, where borrowing went back even before the time of the Prophet Muhammad. In 1954, two years before his death at nearly the same age as that of his teacher Nöldeke, Torrey could still say in a letter written in his clear and beautiful handwriting which showed hardly any traces of his ninety years: "Any study connected with the Qur'ân interests me." In between, there was a life rich in scholarly achievement. He published many careful and ingenious decipher-ments of inscriptions, documents, and legends on coins in Hebrew and Aramaic, even in Pahlavi. He produced editions of Arabic texts which are still admired for their accuracy and the editorial skill displayed in them. Above all, however, he was captivated by the powerful influences of the religious tradition on the intellectual life of the Western world, and his principal interest was concentrated on the holy writings of the three great monotheistic religions.

Early in his career, he concerned himself with the books of Ezra and Nehemiah and the historicity of the documents quoted in them which illuminate a crucial moment in the history of Judaism. Although he always continued his Old Testament studies, he soon turned to the numerous problems of the genesis of the texts assembled in the canon of the New Testament. He championed vigorously the thesis of Aramaic originals from which the Greek Gospels and even the Apocalypse of St. John (Revelation) were translated, and he wrestled with the ancient puzzle of the dates of their composition. His most detailed work dealing with the holy book of Islam is the one before us, and again, it is a work concerned with the genesis, the origins, of a moment of singular importance in the spiritual history of mankind. Torrey's approach to the great religious writings was one of deep and respectful empathy, tempered by an immense learning and a strong appreciation of the indispensability for scholars of a critical common sense that would know no relaxation and tolerate no fuzziness. When he was President of the American Oriental Society at the time the United States entered the First World War, he stressed, in particular, this need for "a profound and sympathetic interpretation of Orientals and their work," to which, in his words, "the atmosphere of oriental studies in the last two or three decades had not been favorable." It was the "knowledge of human life in all its dimensions" which he felt was deepened by the immersion in Near Eastern religious history and which he sought to capture in his writings for himself and for others (*Journal of the American Oriental Society,* XXXVIII, 1938, pp. 110, 114).

In addition to the critical spirit that did not allow itself to be hood-

winked by sacred traditions of religion or scholarship, Torrey inherited above all two characteristic traits from the scholarship of the
century in which he was born and in which his mind was formed.
For one, he showed a meticulous, never flagging concern with all the
sources and documentation available, with gathering and presenting
to the reader all the detailed information that might help to throw
light on a given subject; little escaped him in this respect, and the
student today can still discover many instructive references in all his
publications. In the second place, and, perhaps, more important, he
always took clear-cut, completely unequivocal positions. Forthrightly,
if as a rule patiently, he argued what may be called the extremist side
of a scholarly problem, even when he was fully aware and frankly
acknowledged, as in many passages of the present book, that much
of the evidence at his disposal was highly conjectural and based more
upon speculation than on well-established facts. This is not to imply
that all nineteenth-century scholars without exception were averse to
compromise or that none of them considered withholding judgment
on occasion the better part of wisdom. Obviously, this is far from
being the case. Nöldeke himself is an outstanding example. Faced
with complicated speculations and theories about the obscure origins
and history of the gnostic sect of the Mandaeans, Nöldeke simply remarked: "It may have been so, but maybe, it was entirely different."
By and large, however, doubt was not all too highly prized, and self-
assurance was the hallmark of the important and influential scholar.
Especially the great Biblical scholarship of the period, which was
Torrey's principal training ground, was often proud of knowing what,
to us, seems hardly knowable, and proclaiming it publicly as the
only possible truth. Much of this attitude is gone so thoroughly that
we have trouble to realize that it ever existed, and not so very long
ago. Clear-cut positions are now viewed with considerable suspicion.
The pale light of hesitation and compromise appears to be the one
that casts the most illuminating glow. Torrey rightly objected to the
smug, self-congratulatory assumption of a "sichere Grundlage" for
the theory defended by Wellhausen, Andrae, Ahrens, and others, that

it was Christianity that played the decisive role in the birth of Islam (p. 6). But his own theses instructively summarized in the Preface (p. V f.) make use of such forceful descriptions as "utterly untenable" and "completely refuted," and "doubtless" and "unquestionable" are recurring adjectives. When it comes to points which might possibly be used as arguments against his own theory of the Jewish foundation of Islam, his usual objectivity and scholarly patience run somewhat thin, and he gives the impression of being a little annoyed with the obstreperousness of the evidence. On the face of it, the occurrence of Ethiopic loan words in the Qur'ân indicates contacts with an environment that would appear to have been Christian, and not Jewish. It can be argued that these loan words need not necessarily have reached the Prophet directly, but it would seem that Torrey makes all too short shrift of them (p. 53). To give another example, he also does not disdain to claim arbitrarily that the Qur'ânic term *furqân* must be of Jewish Aramaic origin and cannot go back to Aramaic speaking Christians (p. 48, n. 19), although there is no good reason for such a claim. The Christian Aramaic origin was subsequently defended by scholars such as A. Jeffery, R. Bell, and it would seem, R. Paret in his article on the word in the new edition of the *Encyclopaedia of Islam* (II, p. 949 f.). It is enlightening to compare the scholarly stance of Torrey with that exhibited in the article of the Encyclopaedia. Where Torrey is uncompromising in his defense of the Aramaic meaning of the term as the only one applicable to the Qur'ânic passages in which it occurs, Paret, following Bell, tries hard to superimpose some aspects of an Arabic interpretation upon a basic Aramaic meaning, that is, to combine scholarly insight with traditional data and to do justice to both worlds at the same time.

By their very nature, strong, uncompromising positions in historical scholarship are as a rule vulnerable from many sides. Torrey's well-argued thesis that the documents in the books of Ezra and Nehemiah were not genuine was soon undermined by the discovery in Egypt of original documents from the very same period. This definitely favored the assumption of the historicity of the Biblical texts. An extensive

re-examination of the whole question was stimulated by this discovery, and it can probably be said that majority opinion at the
present time has turned into the direction of considering those documents by and large genuine. The Aramaic origin of the Gospels and
Revelation and their early dating so strongly maintained by Torrey
have proved to be more stubborn problems, but again, subsequent
scholarship has been shying away from Torrey's extremist convictions
in this respect. However, while bold and exposed positions are easy
targets, they also stand out from the rest of the landscape and arouse
the curiosity of inquisitive minds. They are tremendously stimulating
for other scholars, and this holds true of all of Torrey's work, including *The Jewish Foundation of Islam.*

Change and progress in the historical disciplines may result from
new discoveries, or from the re-interpretation of known data, or from
a new way of looking at life that may have had its start somewhere
else but which then spreads over the entire intellectual scene. These
three factors do not operate independently. They do depend upon and
interact with each other. New discoveries may trigger new interpretations; new interpretations may change the general outlook; a new
intellectual climate may spur the search for new material, and so on.
In recent years, our civilization has obviously been moving at a much
accelerated pace. Considerable changes can be expected to have taken
place even within the brief span of a generation that has gone by since
the thirties and to have altered the complexion of many a historical
discipline, including Islamology. If we look around in closely related
fields, we cannot fail to notice that new discoveries have contributed
greatly and quite directly to our knowledge of the Bible and of the
world in which it came into being. One needs only think of the
alphabetic texts from Ugarit (Ras Shamra) written in cuneiform
characters in a Canaanite dialect that bears a striking similarity to the
Hebrew attested from later times. An epic and religious literature
dating from the fourteenth century B.C. whose existence was entirely
unexpected has thus been restored to us. Through their language and
through their contents, the Ugaritic tablets have given us new tools

for a different and more precise understanding of many aspects of the Old Testament. The "Dead Sea Scrolls" are another outstanding example. They came to the attention of scholars just twenty years ago, but by now everybody is aware of the multiple implications of the materials recovered since then from the Dead Sea region for Biblical studies and for the Jewish and Christian history of the two centuries preceding and following the birth of Christianity. Many other, and in their way equally important, discoveries have been made in the Near East. They have vastly enriched our knowledge of the history and the civilizations of the fertile crescent north of Arabia and the settled lands in the Arabian peninsula's southwest corner. Many more can be confidently expected to be made as time goes on and archaeologists are able to search more thoroughly the innumerable and largely untouched spots where skill and luck promise a rich harvest. It is regrettable that for the homeland of Islam in Central Arabia, the situation is by no means as favorable and the outlook is much less cheerful. In fact, no important new material has shown up from that particular area in recent decades. What is worse, it does not seem likely that much or anything will ever be found. It is true that we have become used to many surprises and thus may hope for more, even where reason tells us that the chances are limited. There was nothing to prepare scholars for the finds at Ugarit, and very little indeed to alert them to the possibility of ever discovering anything like the Dead Sea Scrolls. However, the odds are very much against archaeological discoveries to throw an entirely new light upon the history of Mecca and Medina and other regions pertinent to the rise of Muhammad and his religion. As far as is known, no significant excavations have been undertaken, and it is doubtful whether they would yield any results. New literary remains that could provide additional, direct knowledge of pre-Islamic Central Arabia have not made their appearance and may never do so.

Some indirectly pertinent data have come from recent discoveries along the marginal areas of Arabia. We may refer to Torrey's argument in favor of an early settlement of Jews in Arabian caravan cities.

According to this theory, Judaism gained its first firm foothold in the Peninsula around the middle of the sixth century B.C. when close to the final collapse of the Neo-Babylonian Empire, one of its rulers, Nabû-nâ'id (Nabonidus), attempted for a number of years to have the center of his rule shifted away from Babylonia toward ancient Harrân in northern Mesopotamia and far south to the oasis city of Têmâ in remote Arabia (p. 10 ff.). Supplementing, and in some ways superior to, the material with which Torrey was familiar, another cuneiform text was found in Harrân not long ago which has reference to these happenings. The new text mentions the names of a number of Arabian towns, among them for the first time according to our knowledge, the ancient name of Medina, Yathrib (*ya-at-ri-bu*). This was as far to the south as Nabû-nâ'id tells us he ventured, and he states that he spent ten years in those Arabian oasis towns along the caravan route, not returning to his city of Babylon during all this time. The first editor of the Akkadian text, C. J. Gadd, rather dramatically points out "the truly remarkable coincidence of two illustrious fugitives, separated by thirteen (read: eleven, twelve?) centuries, both exiles from their own homes, both expelled in the cause of their religions, both taking refuge in the same city and both returning thence after respectively ten or eight years in partial or complete triumph. Medina has twice been the City of a Prophet" (*Anatolian Studies,* VIII, 1958, p. 84). Nothing is said about Jews in this text and the related documents. Much as we would like to find some reference to them and to their participation in these events, we could hardly expect such a detail, if it indeed existed, to have been found worthy of mention. Furthermore, an episodic character seems to surround the whole affair. It did not constitute a major turning point in Near East politics, nor did it have any lasting major consequences. It would thus seem somewhat hazardous to single out this incident as a crucial juncture in the history of the Jews of Arabia. However, it remains most tempting, as it did for Gadd, to think of the Jews who at the time were experiencing the first serious effects of dispersion, as constituting a group willing beyond others to accompany the Baby-

Ionian king on his wanderings. There is no denying that Torrey's view of this origin of Arabian Judaism still has much to recommend itself and remains substantially correct, even if the new evidence does not really confirm it and there is, we must admit, as little positive proof for it as for any other theory about the pre-history of the Jews of Arabia. It may be noted here in passing that on the contrary, Torrey's slight doubts as to the role of Judaism in South Arabia not long before the coming of Islam (p. 20 f.) are probably not shared by many, if any, scholars today.

New material which proves helpful to us in coming closer to an understanding of the cultural situation in Arabia at the time of the Prophet was discovered by H. D. Colt Jr. in the course of his excavations at ancient Nessana (Nitsana) in the Negeb of Palestine during the years 1935-37. Nessana is a long distance from Central Arabia, and it was much more securely tied to Hellenistic civilization. Its inhabitants, including the large and growing Arab element among them, can be assumed to have been quite different from the Arabs of Mecca and Medina. Nevertheless, the non-literary papyri discovered in Nessana and published by C. J. Kraemer Jr. (*Excavations at Nessana*, III, Princeton 1958) show us how people made their living in an area of limited productivity and depending upon artificial irrigation, what products they knew and used, what trades they practiced, and how much or how little they possessed of higher education or enjoyed of the benefits of civilization in such matters as the availability of physicians. Despite all the differences, the cultural atmosphere of Nessana might have had its rather similar counterpart in Mecca and Medina. At any rate, nothing better has so far shown up for us to picture in our imagination what certain aspects of life might have been like in the cities of the Prophet's Arabia.

New evidence, again not from Central Arabia itself but from the Near Eastern region as a whole, has sharply diminished our certainty as to the precise forms in which Judaism and other religions might have become known to the Prophet. The Dead Sea finds have made it plain for everyone to see what prior to them was a matter of arcane scholarly information, namely, that non-Rabbinic sects of Judaism were very prominent in the early Christian centuries. While they were unable in general to brave and survive the conditions which called for religious unity among Jews, they might well have continued in one form or other a little disturbed existence in less accessible regions. Most of our knowledge about the Judaism of the first millennium comes from Rabbinical sources. Consequently, wherever parallels between statements of the Qur'ân and Jewish ideas and beliefs can be traced, the latter are most likely to be known to us from Rabbinical literature, and we are in no position to tell whether they could not also have formed part of the literary heritage of other groups. Any convincing evidence connecting the beliefs of the Dead Sea and other related Jewish sectarians with data furnished by the Qur'ân has not yet turned up. It should, however, not be left unnoticed that Jewish acquaintance with the name of Nabû-nâ'id—and not only his figure dimly seen through the Nebuchadnezzar of the Book of Daniel—is confirmed through the discovery of an Aramaic *Prayer of Nabonidus,* preserved in a very fragmentary fashion in one of the caves of Qumrân. The name of the king as spelled in the document is not an exact rendering of Nabû-nâ'id or Nabonidus. It has been deciphered to read *Nbny,* perhaps to be vocalized Nab(u)nay. Têmâ is also mentioned in the *Prayer,* and so is a soothsayer who has an important function in it and is specifically identified as Jewish. This interesting text appears to add a little more likelihood to the assumption just discussed that the events of Nabû-nâ'id's reign had indeed a more clearly remembered significance for Jewish history than hitherto recognized, although we still cannot be sure whether this might have extended to the beginnings of an intensive Jewish immigration and settlement in the Arabian Peninsula. While no direct relations have so far been traced between Jewish sectarians and the Qur'ân, the *caveat* against any sort of unqualified identification of the Judaism of Central Arabia in the time of Muhammad with Rabbinical Judaism has become more and more distinct and must not be disregarded.

Another field in which much relevant research has been undertaken in recent years, and at least in part on the basis of newly found material, is Gnosticism. Like mysticism, its unidentical twin, Gnosticism was anything but congenial to scholars of Torrey's generation. It was easily dismissed as abstruse and confused. The drama behind its struggle with the dark recesses of the irrational human mind was not recognized. Our own awareness of the irrational forces preponderant in man has made the study of how the adherents of Gnosticism wrestled with the problem of good and evil increasingly attractive to many in our time. The ways in which Judaism was tinged by the gnostic vogue of the first Christian centuries has been carefully investigated and continues to be studied. Again, this has opened up the possibility at least of another approach toward the religious thought of Muhammad's Jewish contemporaries. Christianity also possessed its gnosticizing followers. It is remarkable that some of them resided along the northern border of Arabia in the sixth and seventh centuries of the Christian era. They wrote down their thoughts in Syriac, and some of what they wrote is preserved. We cannot reject out of hand the possibility that they did influence the Prophet's nascent religious beliefs. Gnosticism proper, represented for us most conveniently by the doctrines and literature of Manichaeism and Mandaism, was a powerful force all over the Western part of the globe in those days. Its involved speculations, a mixture of magical religiosity and science, provided emotional satisfaction for the intellectual elite as much as it dazzled the ordinary man who hoped for greater effectiveness in his quest for salvation in something he was not quite able to grasp. The very feature giving Gnosticism its name, the stress put upon *gnôsis* "recognition" of the eternal truth and the road to salvation, may be reflected in the immense concern shown in the Qur'ân for the concept of "knowledge" as the most important aspect of true belief, with tremendous consequences for the later intellectual history of Islam. It is not easy to explain the intensity of the Prophet's feeling for "knowledge" and his constant use of the term on the basis of his own Arabian experience, and gnostic ideas might have provided for him the first stimulus in this direction. Some minor puzzles of the Qur'ân can also be given rather plausible explanations from gnostic sources. Thus, more weight, it seems, may now be attached to the Qur'ânic references to the Sâbians than Torrey considered justified (p. 3 f.). It is true, we have not yet succeeded in identifying the Sâbians with any known gnostic sect. The only safe statement that can be made on the strength of linguistic appearances is that they were a baptizing sect whose home was possibly somewhere in Babylonia although other regions are not excluded. If they are indeed to be identified with the Mandaeans, we still have to contend with all the uncertainties of Mandaean history. Presently, the theory of the one-time Jewish (Palestinian) origin of the Mandaeans has found new supporters, and while the Mandaeans themselves adopted a pronounced anti-Jewish bias, it has even been thought that the Sâbians of the Qur'ân might have been the same gnostic sect in its more original Jewish form.

All that has been said here and what we have meanwhile learned about the religious situation in Muhammad's Arabia comes down to the fact that our information is now recognized to be too deficient for any categorical *a priori* assumptions as to what the Prophet might have had an opportunity to know or not to know and what particular form of a given religion might have been the one represented by his informants.

Factual evidence has done less to alter the outlook of present-day Islamic scholarship on the origin and later development of Islam than has a general change in the intellectual climate in which we are living. It is unmistakable that an approach concerned primarily with attempts to demonstrate dependence on earlier stages of the historical process is no longer able to command the loyalty of historians and is considered by many rather elementary or even primitive. It is now widely felt, and the feeling is steadily gaining ground, that true historical understanding depends upon the insight into and the detailed analysis of innate psychological factors, or economic "laws," or physical environmental conditions. Important phenomena of history are to be explained by themselves and through themselves, preferably without too much reference to what was before and what came afterwards. The winds of change have naturally affected Islamic studies, too. A contributing factor making them particularly receptive to the new approach has been our greatly increased knowledge of the Muslim sources. It has gone far beyond what was known in the last century in sheer bulk if not in depth, and has made us aware of the vast complexity of Muslim civilization and its fundamental reliance upon its own resources and modes of thought. It is not so very far back in time that Islamic studies were cultivated as an adjunct to Biblical and general Semitic studies. Scholars thus trained were naturally inclined to look for and find parallels and examples of dependence and to consider their work done when they had shown how the earlier Near East had influenced and shaped the "modern" Near East that came into being in 622, the year of the hijrah. Now, the pendulum has swung in the other direction, and, as often happens, it would appear that it has swung rather too far for the exigencies of solid scholarship. Most Islamic scholars of today (though, of course, there are exceptions) do not really know any other Semitic language except Arabic, nor are they truly conversant with or interested in what happened before the coming of Islam. It can be said without doing them injustice that they lack any real appreciation for the insights of a Torrey and do not greatly care for his kind of historical approach. For instance, whether or not Torrey was right in explaining the strange *raqîm* in the Qur'ânic version of the famous legend of the Seven-sleepers as a misreading of the name of the Emperor Decius written in Hebrew or Aramaic script (p. 46 f.), the majority of modern Islamists are likely to reject this suggestion outright, principally because they are unable, and therefore unwilling, to assess its merits or drawbacks.

There is, of course, considerable value in attempts to clarify historical phenomena on their own terms. For their correct evaluation, we must be prepared to know how much there is in them that was new and unprecedented, but in truly important developments, simple causality, even where it can be proved beyond doubt, tends to explain only the shell but not the core. No matter how strong and convincing we may find the evidence for outside influences on Muhammad's spiritual and intellectual formation, it will never satisfactorily explain his success in creating something and transforming it into a lasting force affecting all humanity where others doubtlessly exposed to similar influences never dared to disturb the course of history and remained anonymous. The present mood of Islamic scholars tends toward working out the "original" strain in Muhammad's work rather than his indebtedness to others. In his doctoral dissertation, Torrey's immature submission to the intellectual currents of the time showed itself in his blunt assertion that Muhammad was not original. He even went so far as saying that "lack of originality might almost be called his chief characteristic as compared with other founders of religious systems" (*The Commercial-Theological Terms*, p. 49). Clearly, no founder of a religious system can be assumed to have lived in a vacuum. Merely our own ignorance, which increases the farther back we go in time, appears to give other founders of religious systems the edge over Muhammad as far as originality is concerned. In the present work, Torrey makes ample amends for his youthful error. "Long reflection" and "wise calculation" are said to be the outstanding qualities of Muhammad's mind and work (p. V). He was "a man of very unusual originality and energy" (p. 7). And, in conclusion, Torrey willingly admits that "the originality of the man remains more impressive than his dependence" (p. 132). Subsequent research has gone further along these lines and has tried to work out the elements indicative of the Prophet's "originality" and of the uniqueness of his accomplishment in its time and environment.

There is a danger in the modern attitude which was absent before when the great communications revolution was yet to come and contemporary Islam showed as yet little awareness of Western reconstructions of its past history. I do not have in mind the perpetuation of outdated and meaningless slogans such as that of Islam being a "Christian heresy." It can be heard even today, and it is indeed offensive and indefensible in its implied complete disregard for religious and human realities. What I have in mind is an occasional conscious or unconscious tendency on the part of modern scholars to avoid making statements and reaching conclusions which, no matter how necessary and true they are, may not be welcome to the zealous defenders of a traditional religious outlook. The Holy Book, in particular, is felt to be above criticism, as is only natural and corresponds to the sentiment shown toward the Bible in Judaism and Christianity. It is well known, however, that Muslim theology and traditional practice combined to secure for the Qur'ân an even more exalted position than is accorded to the Bible. The uniqueness and divine eternality of the message transmitted by Muhammad has been one of the most sacred dogmas of Islam. It is therefore repugnant to orthodox Muslims to seek for sources of the Qur'ân and to explain Muhammad's thought in historical terms as his own human creation. If there is agreement or disagreement between the Qur'ân and earlier religious documents, it is the latter that reproduce or distort the revelation which eventually reached Muhammad in its pure form. And not only the religious traditionist but also the nationalist firebrand of today is ready to suspect that attempts to put the events of seventh-century Arabia in their proper historical context are motivated by a desire to diminish the stature of the Prophet, and with it, the stature and aspirations of his present-day followers. As a result, pusillanimous minds among scholars tend to shrink from the forthrightness with which a Torrey took for granted the necessity and appropriateness of the causal historical approach even in the case of the founder of a great living religion. This approach, however, while open to modifications and supplementation, must not be abandoned if progress is to be made in the future. Torrey's book can serve as a strong reminder of its usefulness and, indeed, indispensability in spite of or, perhaps, because of its incidental shortcomings.

Today, however, few scholars will go along with that untrammeled freedom of thought and scholarly speculation which Torrey uses throughout his work vis-à-vis traditional information handed down to us in the large and rich medieval literature. One of his theses proclaims that too great a dependence on the native commentators of the Qur'ân has impeded the exact understanding of it (p. VI). This statement is true. It cannot be repeated often enough that the medieval Muslim scholars, great men and prodigious workers though they were, were not different from modern scholars. On the whole, they were neither better nor worse. Notwithstanding claims they themselves or others often made, they did not have an uninterrupted, fully trustworthy tradition to rely on, and they did not have any special immediate, intimate, or inspired access of their own to the meaning of the Holy Book. They looked at it in the light of their own time-bound vision, learning, and acquired ideas and prejudices, the same way a modern scholar approaches the subjects he wishes to investigate. However, outright rejection of the tradition they created and set down in many books raises an important and tantalizing question. We may ask ourselves how far we should go in making ourselves independent of our medieval predecessors and in relying upon our own acumen, our own thought processes, our own intellectual prejudices. Torrey goes very far indeed in this direction. He delights, it would seem, in revealing that whatever the literary tradition says and tries to establish as historical verity, the very opposite makes sense, too, and to his mind, quite often much better sense. Striking examples are scattered all over the pages of this book. We may note, for instance, the manner in which he tackles the old problem of the extent of the Prophet's education. The tradition of his illiteracy, it is true, does not belong to the articles of faith for which unanimous acceptance was required at all times, but it remained for Torrey to take up and press the case not only for his full literacy in his Arabic mother tongue but also for a possible knowledge—a modest one, to be sure—on his part of Hebrew and Aramaic (p. 36 ff.). Or take the Muslim traditional view on the rather haphazard fashion in which the Qur'ân was preserved and collected after Muhammad's death. The tradition is quite firm in this respect. Torrey is loath to give it much credit. He paints a completely different picture of how the Qur'ân gradually took on the shape of a book under the direction of the

Prophet himself and during his lifetime (p. 92 f.). Scholarship even more than tradition has been inclined to assume that most of the Prophet's detailed knowledge of Judaism dated from the early years of his stay in Medina. Not so Torrey. He is convinced that most of what the Prophet had learned of Jewish history, literature, customs, and law was acquired in Mecca. As a necessary corollary, he maintains that the Jews of Mecca, about whose existence the tradition is silent, departed from Mecca already during his lifetime and thus disappeared from history before they came to the attention of historians (p. 97). Torrey's ingenuity and courage deserve our admiration. They help to open our eyes to the shakiness of the foundations upon which much of our presumed knowledge rests. However, the problem remains. Any comfortable yearning for a blind acceptance of traditional information must be met with continued resistance. But if the tradition is to be rejected and there is no concrete evidence to take its place, it seems most hazardous to invent as it were a tradition of our own resulting from our own reasoning. No matter how good a case may be made for such a new tradition, it will hardly deserve or, at any rate, find general and permanent acceptance. The written word of old exercises too strong a hold over us, and there will always be those who argue that what was written down centuries ago by those closer (though not close) to the events and ideas they discuss should be favored.

Some minor details in Torrey's work could be singled out for correction. Others might be marked as hardly being as unexceptionable as they appear at first sight. If these introductory pages use spellings such as Muhammad and Qur'ân as against Torrey's Mohammed and Koran, this is because the more exact transliterations of the Arabic forms have slowly gained acceptance even outside scholarly circles. Any consistency in this respect is still far from possible or from being practical, as witnessed, for instance, by the spellings Mecca (for which Torrey prefers Mekka, which is something of a hybrid between an "accepted" spelling and an exact transliteration) and Medina. The changed spellings are not meant to imply any criticism. But there are some points proposed or adopted by Torrey that would seem quite doubtful. Thus, the etymology that connects the name of the oasis city of Khaybar with Hebrew *heber* (p. 13) has little to recommend itself. In the meantime, the identity of the first consonant of both words has become more solidly established than it had been before, but this identity goes back to very ancient times. Moreover, the name occurs already in the Nabû-nâ'id inscription from Harrân in the form *khi-ib-ra-a*. If Khaybar were of Hebrew origin, the Jewish connection with the city would antedate the sixth century B.C. by centuries. For historical even more than linguistic reasons, the Hebrew etymology of Khaybar remains a mere guess, and a most unlikely one. Why Yathrib, the original name of Medina, should be of Egyptian origin is hard to fathom. The assumed phonetic similarity with Athribis (p. 13) may be due to the merest chance. The reader may be warned again that the existence of a strong Jewish element in Mecca, postulated on the same page, is entirely conjectural and devoid of any positive confirmation. Claiming Arabic origin for the Mishnaic expression *sphar têrûkhîn* in Gittîn IX, 3 (Gittîn 85b), if this is what Torrey wishes to do (p. 27), appears to be a simple oversight; the word is attested in Aramaic since ancient times. The coincidence of four non-Arabic expressions occurring in a poem by a Jewish contemporary of the Prophet as well as in the Qur'ân is, in my opinion, rather evidence in favor of the unauthentic character of the verses (p. 33). Claiming that the *manner* of fasting observed during the month of Ramadân, that is, abstaining altogether during the day, and eating and drinking after sundown, is specifically Jewish (p. 138) is stretching a point too far, since this is not the really relevant aspect of the fast of Ramadân and the Jewish manner of fasting admits of quite a few variations. On the other hand, there are many suggestions which, though doubtful and hardly to be proved or disproved at the present state of our knowledge, show off Torrey's original mind and the brilliant perfection of his learning to the greatest advantage, such as, for instance, his explanation of the obscure Qur'ânic proper names Shu'ayb and Dhû l-Kifl (p. 71 f.), his combination of the role of the Meccan well of Zamzam with data from Jewish tradition (p. 84 f.), his sharply focussed arguments against the much favored theory of Snouck Hurgronje concerning the significance of the figure of Abraham-Ibrâhîm in Muhammad's thinking (p. 88 ff.), and many other thoughtful and stimulating suggestions.

What about Torrey's main thesis, the Jewish foundation of Islam? The number of arguments assembled in its favor is impressive, and the forcefulness with which they are presented is likely to sway the reader as it must have fascinated those fortunate enough to hear Torrey deliver the original lectures. Yet, I for one am not ready to commit myself to it. I have always thought that Muhammad's early preoccupation with the last day and the life in the other world as well as the personal role he assigned to himself were not characteristically Jewish. If one were to choose here between Jewish or Christian influence, Christian influence seems more likely. I must admit that this is merely an impression, and a very subjective one at that. As has been pointed out before, we do not know what religious ideas were uppermost in the minds of the Arabian Jews of the time, and there are too many unknown factors concerning the religious situation in Arabia to permit any exact fixation of the direction from which the first impetus to found a religion in the Judaeo-Christian tradition might have reached the Prophet. The present skepticism with regard to unequivocal positions, I fear, is fully justified in this instance. The direction from which the Prophet's earliest formative experiences came cannot now be determined with the exactness scholars have the right and the duty to insist upon. But the question must be raised and discussed again and again. Torrey's work contains a good deal that is debatable or even wrong. It may no longer be within the mainstream of Islamic research, and many of today's Islamists may be unrespon-. sive to its approach and its technique. It does, however, make a noteworthy contribution to the discussion of an important problem, even if it does not solve it. It is full of stimulating ideas and sound information. Above all, it is a fine monument to the critical spirit of a great period of scholarship. There is, I believe, nobody interested in the history of human civilization who cannot learn from it, from its inspired failings as well as its shining, not-to-be-forgotten virtues.

FRANZ ROSENTHAL

BIBLIOGRAPHICAL NOTE

The literature on the subject of Muhammad and the Qur'ân published since 1933 is very extensive and could not be listed here, even if this were desirable. A few hints must suffice. English translations of the Qur'ân are those by R. Bell (Edinburgh 1937-39) and A. J. Arberry (London 1955). The most recent scholarly translation is the German translation by R. Paret (Stuttgart 1966). Introductory works on the Qur'ân were published by R. Blachère, *Le Coran* (Paris 1947), in French and by R. Bell, *Introduction to the Qur'ân* (Edinburgh 1953), in English. Among the numerous biographies of Muhammad, one may, in particular, consult the two volumes by W. M. Watt, *Muhammad at Mecca* (Oxford 1953), and *Muhammad at Medina* (Oxford 1956). At the time Torrey was working on his book, a detailed study of the Qur'ânic narratives connected with the Old Testament and Judaism was under preparation by H. Speyer who dated his foreword to the completed volume in 1931. Speyer's work was published under the title of *Die biblischen Erzählungen im Qoran* in Gräfenheinichen around 1938 or 1939, but few copies got into circulation and are preserved. A reprint was published in Hildesheim in 1961. Going beyond the strictly Qur'ânic material are such works as *Judaism in Islam* by A. I. Katsh (New York 1954), or *Ursprung und Entwicklung der arabischen Abraham-Nimrod Legende* by H. Schützinger (Bonn 1961). For *The Foreign Vocabulary of the Qur'ân*, A. Jeffery's book of this title (Baroda 1938), with its very thorough documentation, may be consulted, together with the suggestions on the Iranian elements in the Qur'ânic vocabulary by G. Widengren, *Muhammad the Apostle of God* (Uppsala 1955), pp. 178-198. For the Jews of Arabia, one may, for instance, compare the study by the historian of Arabian Judaism, J. W. Hirschberg, *Jüdische und christliche Lehren im vor- und frühislamischen Arabien* (Cracow 1939), and the same author's Hebrew history of the Jews in Arabia (Tel Aviv 1946, 1957), or I. Ben-Zvi, *Les Origines de l'établissement des tribus d'Israel en Arabie (Le Muséon, LXXIV, 1961, pp.*

143-190). On Jesus and Christianity in the Qur'ân, there exists a voluminous literature, as, for instance, most recently, G. Parrinder, *Jesus in the Qur'ân* (New York 1965), but to my knowledge, none of it is historically oriented. A convenient up-to-date summary in particular of possible gnostic influences upon Muhammad is K. Rudolph, *Die Anfänge Muhammeds im Lichte der Religionsgeschichte (Festschrift W. Baetke,* Weimar 1966, pp. 298-326).

PREFACE

When, in consultation with President Wise and Dr. Kohut, I chose this subject for the Lectures on the Stroock Foundation, I did so partly because of my belief, long held, that some important matters relating to Mohammed and the Koran are in need of a fresh examination; partly also in the conviction that the Arabian prophet and his marvellous book are in themselves of such great interest that even a somewhat technical discussion may be given a hearing by the layman. The subject has a certain timeliness by reason of the many recent investigations in its field, and also because of the presence of new material relating to conditions in ancient Arabia.

Among the conclusions which are given especial prominence in the Lectures, the following may be mentioned.

The Jewish colonies in the Hijaz were established by a very considerable migration, chiefly from Palestine, in the sixth century B.C. Both Dozy and August Müller saw the plain evidence of a large migration of Jews from Palestine into northern Arabia, but neither was able to find a convincing reason for such a movement. A most suitable occasion is now seen to have been given by a remarkable episode in neo-Babylonian history.

The orthodox Muslim dogma that Mohammed was an unschooled man is utterly untenable, though even the most recent treatises continue to give it some credence.

The Arabian prophet is less mysterious than he has generally been regarded (every great genius, to be sure, is more or less of a mystery). He was at all times sincere, never doubting that the self-hypnotism which he had learned to produce, and which he continued to practise at critical times, brought him a divine revelation. His *naiveté* is commonly exaggerated by modern interpreters and made to explain too much; very often what seems merely childlike is the result of long reflection and wise calculation.

XXVII

The doctrine that the foundation of Islam was mainly Christian has held the field for nearly half a century. It is completely refuted, however (as I think will appear), partly by evidence which the Koran furnishes, partly also by material gathered from pre-Mohammedan Arabia.

The "higher criticism" of the Koran has suffered from undue dependence on the native commentators. Certain theories too hastily propounded by the greatest European authorities in this field have dominated all subsequent research.

"Islām" began with Ishmael, the father of the Arabs. It was thus by right primarily *an Arabian religion,* even though Ishmael's sons had rejected it. Mohammed's account of the Sacrifice (Sura 37: 100 ff.) is very skilfully managed.

The Lectures were delivered in March, 1931, but for various reasons it was not found practicable to publish them at once. Lectures I, IV, and V are given here very nearly in the form in which they were delivered. Lectures II and III, as they are here published, show a very considerable expansion and rearrangement, each containing an amount of material which is too technical to be inflicted on a popular audience.

It is a source of regret that some books from which I could have received instruction have not been accessible to me. I am especially sorry that Professor Rostovtzeff's *Caravan Cities* came to hand too late for my use.

The verses of the Koran are cited (as is now customary) according to the numbering in Flügel's edition. Semitic names and words generally familiar are not transliterated exactly, but are given in their popular form. Citations not strictly verbal are indicated by single quotation marks.

It remains to tender hearty thanks to the Bloch Publishing Company for the care which they have bestowed on the typography of the volume and on all the details of its publication.

CHARLES C. TORREY

May, 1933

CONTENTS

FIRST LECTURE

THE JEWS IN ARABIA

The question of the chief source, or sources, of Mohammedanism has long been discussed, and quite recently has called forth a number of scholarly investigations throwing new light on this or that feature of the subject.[1] The Arabian prophet himself declared Islam to be the true heir of the old Hebrew revelation—in which term he would include also the New Testament. Whether it can be said in some true sense that Mohammedanism grew out of Judaism, may appear in the progress of these lectures. It is fitting that this Jewish Institute of Religion should give the opportunity, through the medium of the Stroock Foundation, for a new treatment of the subject by a representative of the other great religion which traces its origin to the Israelite faith.

The history of Islam is of great interest in every part, but most of all in its beginnings. What we are now called upon to notice is not that it is the religion of some 200 millions of men, but that its inception was in remarkable degree the work of one man; of whose life, private and public, we have a considerable amount of definite knowledge. Its sacred

---

[1] [The following, especially, have appeared during the past decade. Guidi, *L'Arabie antéislamique*, Paris, 1921. W. Rudolph, *Die Abhängigkeit des Qorans von Judentum u. Christentum*, 1922. Lammens, *La Mecque à la Veille de l'Héjire*, Beyrouth, 1924. D. S. Margoliouth, *The Relations between Arabs and Israelites prior to the Rise of Islam*, 1924. Snouck-Hurgronje, "Der Islam" (in *Lehrbuch der Religionsgeschichte*, ed. Bertholet u. Lehmann), 1924. R. Roberts, *The Social Laws of the Qorān*, London, 1925. J. Horovitz, *Koranische Untersuchungen*, 1926; also "Jewish Proper Names and Derivatives in the Koran," *Hebrew Union College Annual*, II (1925), 145–227. R. Bell, *The Origin of Islam in its Christian Environment*, London, 1926. Tor Andrae, *Der Ursprung des Islams u. das Christentum*, Uppsala u. Stockholm, 1926. De Lacy O'Leary, *Arabia before Muhammad*, 1927. K. Ahrens, "Christliches im Qoran," ZDMG., IX (1930), 15–68, 148–190.]

book, the Koran, was his own creation; and it lies before us practically un-
changed from the form which he himself gave it. We thus seem to know
the origins of Mohammedanism much more intimately than those of any
other world faith. There is another side, however, and the serious problems are many, even here at the outset. The man and the book stand out
pretty clearly to our view, but the surroundings are badly blurred. We
know very little about the Mekka of that day, and we have scant information regarding either the materials or the processes by whose aid a great
religion was then coming into being. Apparently a root out of dry ground,
an Arabian religion intended for Arabs, it nevertheless was designed and
expected by its founder to conquer the world. There was behind this confidence more than mere self-assurance, more than pride in the Koran
and trust in Muslim armies. Mohammed firmly believed that the new
faith was an old faith, and that its evident foundations went far outside
Arabia.

It did indeed sweep over all Western Asia, Egypt, North Africa, and a
portion of Europe, in an incredibly short time. We can see certain external reasons for this: the impetus of an awakened race, whose country
was already too narrow; and the comparative weakness of the civilized
nations which were encountered. More important still, however, was the
driving power inherent in the new religion itself. Where did the cameleer
of Mekka get the materials of the faith which set the neighboring world
on fire, and which today, after thirteen centuries, is the religion of many
peoples and parts of the earth?

Unquestionably the first impression gained by a reader of the Koran
is that Mohammed had received the material of his new faith and practice mainly from the Jews of the Hijaz. On almost every page are encountered either episodes of Hebrew history, or familiar Jewish legends, or
details of rabbinical law or usage, or arguments which say in effect that
Islam is the faith of Abraham and Moses. It is natural to suppose that all
this was ultimately derived from Israelites; and that these Israelites were
Mohammed's own neighbors is the unescapable impression constantly
produced by his language: he is speaking to those who were within reach
of his voice, not to far distant or imaginary hearers.

These facts, if taken by themselves, would obviously indicate that the Arabian prophet's religious education had been thoroughly Jewish. Even so, we should be reduced to conjecture as to the details of the process: how, and in what form, he obtained his instruction; what teachers and what means of teaching were available. But there are many more facts to be taken into account. Islam is a fusion of diverse elements, some easily identified, others of obscure origin. The Koran contains a considerable contribution from Arabian paganism, which Mohammed adopted, whether by his own choice or under constraint. The borrowing from the native heathendom is usually obvious enough, and yet even here some things are doubtful. There is also in the Koran a distinctly Christian element; how pervasive and how important, is at present a subject of controversy. Its sources have been even more problematic than those of the Jewish teaching.

Abraham Geiger's brilliant little study, *Was hat Mohammed aus dem Judenthume aufgenommen?*, 1833 (reprinted in 1902), held the field for many years, even after the progress of Islamic studies had left it far behind. There followed a reaction in favor of Christianity as the main source of Mohammed's inspiration. To this, the great influence of Wellhausen gave an impetus which has been lasting. In his *Reste arabischen Heidentums*, 1887, 204–212, he treated briefly the origin of Islam, which he held to be prevailingly Christian, employing arguments which at the present day seem surprisingly weak throughout. He was influenced especially by the fact that Mohammed's converts were at first called "Sābi'ans" by the Mekkans. Since much has been made of this fact in recent years, it will not be out of place to notice it briefly here. The Sabians (otherwise known as the Mandaeans) were a Gnostic sect in southern Babylonia. There was constant traffic across the desert from Irak to Mekka, and the existence of this sect was perhaps known to many in the Hijaz. When Mohammed awoke to the fact of great religions in the world, his interest was very naturally aroused by the report of this ancient community, belonging neither to Judaism nor to Christianity, and yet bearing a certain resemblance to both. His knowledge of its existence was very possibly gained from his Mesopotamian Jewish instructor, who will be mentioned frequently in the subsequent lectures. He mentions the Sabians several times in the Koran (22:17; 2:59; 5:73); [2] and in view of his fondness for strange names and words, especially in the early part of his career, they might be expected to appear oftener. The Mekkans heard the name from Mohammed, and it provided them with a very convenient epithet, used of course derisively. That they did in fact thus employ it, is attested not only by several passages in Ibn Hisham's Life of the Prophet, but also by an undoubtedly contemporary record, the verses of Surāqa ibn 'Auf ibn al-Aḥwaṣ (Aghani XV, 138), in which he rallies the poet Lebid on his conversion.

The only point of connection between Mohammedans and Sabians which Wellhausen is able to find lies in the fact that the latter were baptists, while Islam prescribed certain washings. He remarks (p. 206): 'The five prayers and ablutions go back to the very earliest Islamic time, and Mohammed laid great weight on them.' This, however, can hardly stand as evidence. The five prayers are later than the Koran; and as for the relatively simple ablutions, it seems clear that they were merely derived from Jewish custom. These matters will be considered later. As for Mohammed and the Sabians, I am in full agreement with Bell, *op. cit.*, 148, that it is "extremely improbable that he knew anything about them." [3] The Koran mentions the Magians of Persia in one passage (22:17), and here also it is probable that he knew hardly more than the name.

Wellhausen's verdict nevertheless remains in force. It is quoted with approval, and with repetition of his several arguments, in Nöldeke-Schwally, *Geschichte des Qorāns*, I, 7 f. H. P. Smith, *The Bible and Islam* (New York, 1897), accepts the demonstration, and asserts (p. 315), "The impulse came from Christianity." Rudolph, *Die Abhängigkeit u. s. w.*, 63–71, elaborates the arguments, and generally expresses himself cautiously, but remarks (p. 67), "Nach alledem ist die Richtigkeit der These Wellhausens kaum zu bezweifeln." Many others follow in the same track,

---

[2] [In 5:73 perhaps interpolated; note the nominative case!].

[3] [The "parallels" between Islam and Sabianism set forth by St. Clair Tisdall in his very useful little volume, *The Original Sources of the Qur'ān* (London, 1911), pp. 52 ff., are all derived from a Muslim writer whose imagination filled the existing gap in the customary manner].

asserting that the influence of Christianity was more potent than that of Judaism in starting Mohammed on the course which he followed; giving him the outlines of his conception of a new religion and providing him with the essentials of its material. Many of those elements which on their face appear to be manifestly of Israelite origin are explained as properties which had been taken over by the Christians and came through them to the Arabian prophet.

This latter argument can be turned the other way with at least equal force. The two religions, Judaism and Christianity, had much in common in that day; each had continued to exercise some influence on the other. Jews had some knowledge of Christian literature, and *vice versa*. There are in the Koran numerous passages in regard to which one might say (and some scholars actually have said): "Here is distinctly Christian doctrine"; or even, "Here is a saying plainly suggested by such and such a verse of the New Testament." Another, with equal justification, could claim the same utterances as showing Israelite influence, and find equally close parallels in the Hebrew scriptures. In not a few such cases the religious conception, and even the formula in which it is expressed, can be found in the pagan religious records of Western Asia, centuries before Islam and independent even of Hebrew thought. Men think alike, and religious ideas in particular bud and blossom in linguistic forms which admit of no great variation. Mere verbal resemblances, even when close and extended, are likely to mislead the one who is looking for them. Very much that is easily included in a collection of "parallel passages" may be as easily excluded as due to inevitable coincidence in human thought and speech. When such a collection is once undertaken it is hard to find a stopping place, and the grains of wheat are soon buried under the bushels of chaff. I confess to having brought away such an impression of fruitless abundance from my reading of the exhaustive study by Ahrens, "Christliches im Qoran" (mentioned above). Rudolph's far briefer and well chosen list of "parallels" (10–17) likewise affords no evidence that the prophet had ever become acquainted with any portion of the N. T. scriptures; and his own sound and well stated conclusions (18 ff.) deserve careful reading.

I have been unable, in spite of continued efforts, to get sight of Andrae's book. From the extensive use of it by Ahrens, however, in the
publication just mentioned, it is possible to see the manner, and in part
the material, of his argument. The latter author (p. 18) quotes Andrae's
main conclusions, to the effect that ' "die eschatologische Frömmigkeit
des Qorans auf das nächste mit der religiösen Anschauung verwandt ist,
die in den syrischen Kirchen vor und zur Zeit Muhammeds herrschte";
"die Predigt (des Qorans) hat bestimmte Vorbilder in der syrischen Lit-
eratur"; wir finden im Qoran "nicht nur die religiösen Gedanken, son-
dern in mehreren Fällen sogar die homiletischen Formeln und fest-
stehende erbauliche Redewendungen," wie sie uns bei den syrischen
Schriftstellern entgegentreten.' Ahrens concludes (ibid.): "Damit ist der
Qoranforschung, soweit es sich um den Anteil des Christentums an der
Entstehung des Islams handelt, eine sichere Grundlage gegeben."

On the contrary, the foundation just described, so far from being
"sicher," is of the most insecure and unsatisfactory character. The religious and moral exhortations of the Koran are in the main of very general
application, and are expressed in terms which could be paralleled in any
literature of popular instruction. The ideas expressed (except for the frequent polemic against the Christian Trinity) are those which were common to all the principal religions and sects, Jewish, Christian, and Gnostic (all more or less syncretistic) in that time and part of the world. There
certainly is no safe ground for saying (as some have said): 'This Koranic
teaching is Gnostic,' or 'This is Manichaean'—in our dense ignorance of
the type of Christianity that was known in the Hijaz, and especially, the
type of Judaism that was actually present in Mekka in Mohammed's time,
and from which we know him to have derived such a very large proportion of what we find in the Koran. The general knowledge of certain
Christian doctrines, and of specific Christian terms, was much more widespread in Arabia in the prophet's time than the scholars of a former generation realized. New evidence has been collected, as will appear. The most
of the catchwords and other characteristic properties which Mohammed
has been credited with introducing to his fellow-countrymen are now seen
to have been well known to them before his day. "Christliches im Qoran"

there is, indeed, and that in considerable amount; but the question of its origin has hardly been brought nearer to settlement by recent discussions.

Ahrens sees reason for believing that Mohammed received his teaching, now from Arians (pp. 154 f.), now from Nestorians (18, 173), and again from Gnostics and Manichaeans (15, 18, 167). Christian hermits, presumably in the Hijaz, told him what to say (186). His slaves, doubtless from Abyssinia and Syria (these of course Monophysite), gave him the continuous instruction which he needed (187 f.). Mohammed's New Testament material, he decides, is taken from nearly every part of the Christian scriptures: Gospels, Acts, Pauline Epistles, and the Book of Revelation (172 f.).

Certainly to many students of the Koran this equipment of the Arabian prophet will seem excessive, and the supposed course of training a bit bewildering. I shall endeavor to show, in subsequent lectures, that in the Koran itself there is no clear evidence that Mohammed had ever received instruction from a Christian teacher, while many facts testify emphatically to the contrary; and that, on the other hand, the evidence that he gained his Christian material either from Jews in Mekka, or from what was well known and handed about in the Arabian cities, is clear, consistent, and convincing.

It is quite fruitless to attempt to distinguish between Jewish and Christian religious teaching at the outset of Mohammed's career on the simple ground of essential content, naming the one or the other as that which exercised the original and determining influence ("den *entscheidenden* Einfluss," Rudolph, 65) over him at the time when his religious ideas began to take shape. The doctrines which fill the earliest pages of the Koran: the resurrection, the judgment, heaven and hell, the heavenly book, revelation through the angel Gabriel, the merit of certain ascetic practices, and still others, were quite as characteristically Jewish as Christian. Mohammed was a thoughtful man, and, in addition, a man of very unusual originality and energy. The "initial impulse" came from his early and continued contact with representatives of "a religion" far superior to Arabian paganism, ultimately representative also of a higher civilization. He lived among Israelites, and knew much about them. He had seen

Christians, and heard more or less in regard to them. At first and for some time he thought of the Christians as a Jewish sect which had begun well, but eventually had gone wrong. In the Mekkan Suras of the Koran Jews and Christians form essentially a single class. After his break with the Jews, in the Medina period, he gave some particular attention to the Christians, in contrast with the Jews. Even then, it is plain that he knew very little about them, and the most of what he did know he had received at second hand. Indeed, his acquaintance with either their history or their doctrines is surprisingly slight and superficial. I trust that it will appear, as our discussion proceeds, that while Mohammed's "Islam" was undoubtedly eclectic, yet both in its beginning and in its later development by far the greater part of its essential material came directly from Israelite sources; for, as I shall endeavor to show, the evidence that he had a wide and intimate acquaintance with Judaism is overwhelming in its amount and character.

By "Islam," in the title of these lectures, I mean the Islam of the prophet himself. The prime source therefore, indeed almost the only Arabic source, for our present study is the Koran. The Muslim Tradition (*hadīth*) gives a picture of this primitive period which is so untrustworthy in its religious content that it very rarely can be given any weight. The only safe course is to leave it out of account. Christian and pagan historians and geographers have almost nothing to contribute to our knowledge of this particular time and place. The South Arabian inscriptions give some useful information, as will be seen, in regard to pre-Mohammedan beliefs, though it touches our subject but indirectly. At some points of truly high importance we unfortunately are obliged to depend mainly on conjecture. One of these is no less a subject than the origin and true character of the nominally Israelite communities with which Mohammed came in contact. There are interesting and perplexing questions here, which never have been satisfactorily answered: Who these Israelites were; whence they came; when and how they formed their settlements in western Arabia; what degree of civilization they maintained, and how true a type of Judaism they represented. Some of the numerous replies which have been

made to these and similar queries will be noticed presently. At the time
when Geiger wrote his illuminating little book (mentioned above), no
one doubted the presence of a genuine and authoritative Jewish tradition in Mekka and Medina. At the present time, this is very commonly
doubted, or denied.

Some things become obscure when the searchlight is turned upon
them. Certainly the average student of Koran, Bible, Talmud, and Midrash could easily receive the impression that rabbis and scribes, experts
in halacha and haggada, and well informed laymen besides, had for a
considerable time been close to Mohammed's ear, and continued to be
within reach of his tongue. He persistently attacks the "people of the
Book" in a way that shows unmistakably that he thought of them as acquainted, one and all, with their scriptures. It is their *knowledge* that
impresses him, and their refusal to receive him and his "Muslims" into
their privileged circle that exasperates him. What he is lashing is a real
Israelite community, close at hand, not a distant or imaginary learned
people. Yet we hear it said repeatedly, in these days, that there *were* no
genuinely Jewish settlements in Mekka and Medina. What has become
of them? The "loss of the Ten Tribes" has a worthy counterpart in this
puzzle. I have a theory to propound here as to the origin and character of
these Israelite neighbors of the Arabian prophet. Its validity can best be
judged after the material of the remaining lectures has been presented.

It might seem to us strange that Israelites in any large number should
have chosen to settle in the Hijaz. We might indeed expect to find them
in some other parts of Arabia, even at an early date. Yemen was always
a rich country; and if the Queen of Sheba could come to Solomon, Hebrew merchants could make their way to the Sabaean mountain cities.
There were emporia in northeastern Arabia, on the Persian Gulf, comparatively easy of access, which might seem attractive to any who could
enjoy a continuing summer temperature of 120° Fahrenheit (or more) in
the shade. But the considerations which would lead even adventurous
traders and colonists to migrate with their families into the remote wilder-
ness of perpetual sand and scanty oases east of the Red Sea are at first
sight not so obvious.

There was good reason, however, for the choice; though only vigorous and enterprising men would be moved by it. From time immemorial an important trade route had passed through the narrow coastal strip on the western side of the great peninsula. This was for many centuries a highway of commerce between India and eastern Africa on the one hand, and the cities of Palestine, Syria, and Asia Minor on the other hand. The Greek historians tell of the lively traffic, and in Ezekiel 27:19-22 we have a catalogue of the wares which were brought from Yémen to the city of Tyre. Eventually the Roman shipping through the Red Sea, with its lower freight charges, dealt a severe blow to the camel express line, whose business temporarily declined. For various reasons, certain emporia of Yemen fell into insignificance, or even into ruin. Great changes in the commercial centers of gravity, due to new phases of the Roman colonial policy, had their effect on the traffic of this route. Petra was abandoned, Palmyra not rebuilt. Other cities along the great highway, east of the Jordan and the Sea of Galilee, found that the days of their prosperity were numbered. But the old trade route never lost its importance, and what is more, its great days were not over.

How early, may we suppose, were Hebrew settlements to be found in northern Arabia? Perhaps as far back as the seventh century B.C., when the main dispersion was beginning; perhaps even earlier; there is nothing to make the supposition impossible. History shows the Hebrews always pushing out, and far out, along the arteries of commerce, after their eyes had once been opened to the opportunities in foreign lands. But it seems very unlikely that any Hebrew trading settlements worthy of the name should have arisen in western Arabia before the time when Jerusalem was devastated by the armies of Nebuchadrezzar.

Now it happens that there was an extraordinary reason why merchants in large number should have been attracted to Arabia in the last years of the Chaldaean period and immediately thereafter. Cuneiform documents, recently discovered, have given us a glimpse of a surprising little chapter of western Asiatic history of which we had hitherto been in almost total ignorance. For reasons which we can only partially conjecture, the neo-Babylonian king Nabonidus transferred his royal residence to the city of Teima, near the northern border of the Hijaz.[4] His son, Belshazzar, was left in charge of Babylon. The main facts, as far as they are now known, are excellently set forth in Professor Dougherty's volume entitled *Nabonidus and Belshazzar,* published by the Yale University Press in 1929. The name of the city is familiar in the Bible. In Gen. 25:15 Teima is one of the descendants of Ishmael. The city as an important trading station is mentioned in Is. 21:14 and Jer. 25:23; Job 6:19 speaks of "the caravans of Teima." The oasis, with its remarkable water supply, could support a considerable population; and the prestige given to it by the residence of the Great King helped to make it not only the most important point in the famous artery of commerce, but also a cosmopolitan center. This seems well illustrated in the Aramaic inscribed stele of Teima, now in the Louvre. It is a votive monument, set up in the temple of an Aramaic deity. The priest who erected it has an Assyrian name, but the name of his father is Egyptian. The date of the monument is probably the early part of the fifth century B.C.

One reason, at least, why Nabonidus chose Teima for his royal residence is easy to see. The city was, and had long been, the junction of great trade routes. At this point the line of traffic from Yemen through the Hijaz to Syria was crossed by the line which ran through the desert from Egypt to Mesopotamia—a route which the Babylonian monarch doubtless wished to improve, as well as to control. Another important caravan track ran from Teima around through Ha'il and Riad to Gerrha on the Persian Gulf. And finally, a part of the merchandise that was brought up through the Red Sea by boat or raft, after being landed at Yenbo or Aila was brought to this distributing center.[5] After the Great King had taken his eventful step, there was not. in all Western Asia an opportunity of promising colonization comparable to the one offered by the oases of Teima and the northern Hijaz. It was not the call of a temporary condition, but the sure promise (fulfilled in the event) of a permanently prosperous development.

[4] [Strictly speaking, Teima was not in the Hijaz, though it is often thus included for convenience].

[5] [For the main sources of our knowledge of this traffic, see for example De Lacy O'Leary, *Arabia before Islam,* pp. 53 f., 72, 79, 103–106, and the notes].

After the destruction of the temple at Jerusalem and the devastation of Judea by the Chaldaeans, in the year 586, the Jews of all that region were temporarily scattered. Some groups migrated to more remote lands, especially to those cities where Jewish colonies were already in existence; other companies doubtless returned to the neighboring regions on the east and south, to Moab, Ammon, and Edom, where they had taken refuge a few months earlier, as we are told in Jeremiah, chapters 40–43. Others, probably a large number, retired to Egypt (2 Kings 25:26). We certainly may take it for granted that all the loyal Jews in this temporary dispersion wished to see Jerusalem restored, and that very many of them returned as soon as the way was open; on this whole difficult subject I may refer to my *Ezra Studies,* pp. 297–301. But whatever may have been the conditions in Jerusalem and Judea in the years immediately subsequent to the catastrophe, and especially after the death of Nebuchadrezzar, in the year 561, we can now for the first time see with certainty the conditions of a very important migration of Jews into northwestern Arabia.

Nabonidus reigned from 555 to 538 B.C. Was Teima destined to be the residence of other Babylonian kings? Whether or no, the eyes of all the neighboring world were turned to that city, and to the new opportunities of traffic in its vicinity. The Arabs were not a people capable of taking full advantage of what was offered; the call was obviously for outsiders, and it sounded loudest in Palestine and the countries east and south of the Dead Sea, in Syria, and in Egypt. Among all those who could hear and heed, there were none more likely to enter and take possession of the field than the recently expatriated Jews. I think we may regard it as certain that the Jewish settlements in the Hijaz, which we find so flourishing in the time of Mohammed, were established at this early date, the latter half of the sixth century B.C., under the impulse here described. I shall presently give further reason for this belief. If this origin of certain large colonies is assumed, we may take it for granted that they suffered many changes, through increment (especially), loss, and other shifting conditions, during the many centuries from which we have no record of their existence. There was good reason for their prosperity, for the caravan trade between Yemen and the northern lands was always active, and (as we have seen) there was other traffic inside Arabia and across the desert to Babylonia.

South of Teima, the next important station on the great route is the oasis of Khaibar. This is known to us as a very prosperous Jewish settlement, and it is reasonable to suppose that it was founded at this same time. The name is very likely Hebrew, an Arabic variation of *Kheber*, "community" (Margoliouth, *Mohammed*, pp. 355 f.). It was reputed the richest city of the Hijaz. The settlement was raided by Mohammed and his followers in the seventh year of the hijra, as a sort of consolation prize after the humiliating failure of the attempt of the Muslims to enter Mekka. The Koran (48, 18 f.) boasts of "a victory and great booty"; and in fact the plunder was enormous.

About one hundred miles farther south lay the city of Yathrib (later known as Medina). Here, again, the Jewish colonists entered, and eventually constituted a large and very important part of the population. It does not seem to be the case that they *founded* Yathrib, as is sometimes asserted, nor even that they were among the earliest settlers in that city. This place at all events must have been from time immemorial a station of primary importance on the caravan route. The city lies in a very fertile and well watered valley, and has convenient access to the Red Sea at Yenbo. The name Yathrib is apparently Egyptian, identical with the well known city-name Athribis. In the time of Mohammed, the Jews constituted three separate communities, two of them occupying strongly fortified positions outside the city. The fate of these three tribal communities, under Mohammed's displeasure, is well known. Two of the tribes were plundered and banished, and the men of the third were butchered.

Some three hundred miles south of Yathrib (that is, Medina) lay the cities of Mekka and Ṭā'if. There is no evidence that the latter city ever contained an important Jewish settlement. Mekka, on the contrary, contained in the time of Mohammed a strong Jewish element, to whose existence the Koran gives abundant and unimpeachable witness. We have no direct testimony, worthy of credence, as to the antiquity of the settlement. The fanciful tales told by the Arab traditionists are all worthless for our purpose. As in the case of the settlements at Teima, Khaibar, and Yathrib,

we must content ourselves with indirect evidence, aided by conjecture. I
think it will ultimately be recognized as probable that all four of these
Jewish settlements were constituted in the same early period, primarily
as commercial enterprises, under the impulse just described. If there really
was a Hebrew colonizing movement southward along the Arabian trade
route in the day of Teima's glory, the stream of migration cannot have
stopped short of Mekka. That city, presumably as old as the caravan traffic through the Hijaz, must have been important as early as the sixth
century B.C., though perhaps not for all the reasons which can be given
for its paramount influence in the Arabia of Mohammed's day. At this
latter time, Mekka was the principal meeting point for the Arabian tribes;
which resorted thither, not so much because of the renowned sanctuary,
and the rites connected with it, as because of the great opportunity of inter-
tribal trade afforded by the sacred territory and the sacred months. Long
before the rise of Islam, indeed, Mekka had been famed for its open mar-
ket. It was also known for its hospitality to any and every variety of
Arabian superstition. During all the time (of duration unknown to us) in
which it possessed a truly central sanctuary, its people would doubtless
have been undisturbed by the entrance of a foreign faith. Israelite settlers
might well have been molested on religious grounds at Yathrib, and certainly would have been at Ṭā'if (where nevertheless there was a Jewish
settlement); but at Mekka they would have been tolerated.

As has already been remarked, the caravan trade through the Hijaz had
its ups and downs. All through the Persian and Greek periods of west
Asiatic history it was flourishing. In the middle of the first century of the
present era came the epoch-making discovery by Hippalus of the regular
alternation of the monsoons; and soon after, the *Periplus* was compiled,
putting the navigation around the southern coast of Arabia and through
the Indian Ocean on a new and safe basis. These things, especially, led
to such a development of Roman shipping in the Red Sea that the land
traffic was for a time considerably diminished. The commerce by sea between India and Egypt, which also in the time of the Ptolemies had been
in the hands of the Arabs and the Abyssinians, was now taken over by
the Romans. The South Arabian tribes were chiefly affected by the new

conditions, and at this time began a considerable migration northward, extending even to the northern border of the Syrian desert. Under Byzantine rule, however, especially from the time of Justinian onward, the shipping was neglected, and prosperity returned to the caravan routes. During this favored era, which included the lifetime of Mohammed, Mekka gained in importance, and attracted new immigrants. Among these, if I interpret the Koran rightly, were Jews, one of whom is given very significant mention by the prophet.

The theory of Israelite colonization thus far sketched implies a very extensive migration from the north; and indeed, any migration at the time and under the conditions supposed would naturally have been extensive. Arabia was not a safe destination for small companies of exiles traveling with their wives and children and their household goods. The theory would easily account for the reported size and influence of the Jewish settlements of the Hijaz in Mohammed's day, in view of the wide interval of time, the occasional increase from later migrations, and the added likelihood that Arab tribes professing Judaism were incorporated in considerable number. It would also establish the antecedent probability that these Israelites continued to preserve the faith and the culture of their ancestors. As to this, more presently. We may now take account of other theories which have been propounded in regard to these Jewish-Arab tribes and cities.

This has been a very enticing field for conjecture. The Arab historians found plenty of material with which to operate: genealogies extending from their own day back to Adam; lively anecdotes of Hebrew patriarchs who entered the history of Arabia; movements of Jewish tribes; names and precise details of Israelite personages and communities. European historians of course recognized the worthlessness of much of this information, especially in the field of remote antiquity, though even here there was strong temptation to find something usable. Dozy's very learned and ingenious, but also very fanciful essay entitled *Die Israeliten zu Mekka*, now rarely referred to, gave an extreme example of conjecture based on supposed tradition; though having the merit of employing extra-Arabian sources, and of supposing a real Hebrew migration, however small. His thesis, based largely on 1 Chron. 4:38–43, was that portions of the tribe of Simeon, moving southward from the time of David and especially in the reign of Hezekiah, settled in northern Arabia and formed the nucleus of the colonies found so many centuries later in the Hijaz. Dozy's compatriot, J. P. N. Land, added the conjecture that Simeon was an Ishmaelite tribe which had temporarily joined the Hebrews. No form of the theory, however, could either survive the criticism of 1 Chronicles (to say nothing of the Arab sources employed) nor account for the size and character of the settlements. Later writers, realizing the absence of trustworthy material in all this, made no further use of it.

A too easy-going treatment of the question supposed that Jewish traders and small trading groups had continued to sift down into Arabia, taking up their abode in one after another of the principal stations; until, whether through long continued influx or through the adoption of Judaism by native tribes, they had become so numerous in this or that place that their culture and their religion could make an impression on their Arab neighbors. As to the superiority of genuine Hebrew culture over that of the native tribes of the Hijaz, even in the larger cities, there can of course be no question. It may also be granted that the impression of culture and religion which a community can make on its environment depends more on the quality of those who make up the community than upon their number. But it is quite certain, an undisputed fact, that in the principal cities of the Hijaz, in Mohammed's time, a very large portion of the population professed Judaism. What manner of Israelites were these? Even if the supposed companies of merchants included many of the better class, such as would wish to maintain the traditions of Palestinian civilization, it seems very unlikely that in a gradual process of immigration they could naturally form communities distinct from their surroundings. Yet we have to account for a number of *Jewish tribes,* and at least one Jewish city. No succession of mere trading ventures could possibly explain what we see. Hence arises the question of proselyting; whether it is likely to have been undertaken on a large scale by Jewish traders in Arabia, and whether from its probable result could be explained the condition which we find. The hypothesis of native clans converted through propaganda has played a foremost part in some recent discussions, as a way of accounting for the origin and the apparent character of the nominally Israelite population. The discussion of this question may be reserved for the present: whether it can reasonably be held that these undeniably large and influential Jewish settlements consisted mainly of native Arab tribes which had been converted to a more or less superficial Judaism.

August Müller, *Der Islam im Morgen- und Abendland,* I, 36 f., has some well considered remarks on the general subject. 'Yathrib, like a large part of the northern Hijaz, was in the hands of the Jews. When and whence they had colonized the land, no one knows. Probably it was by fugitives from the Roman-Jewish wars, since it would be hard to suppose an earlier time. For, in spite of their having adopted the Arab ways of life and thought so completely, they still retained their religion and some special peculiarities, which in the course of many centuries they would have been obliged to give up. They spoke among themselves a peculiar Jewish Arabic.' (This last sentence is worthy of especial attention, even though the means of proving and illustrating the fact are very scanty.) As for the *date* which Müller suggests for the colonization, it must be pronounced extremely improbable. This was a time when conditions in the Hijaz were quite uncertain, when all western Asia knew that the caravan traffic was declining, when Yemenite tribes were moving northward into Palestine and Syria because of hard times. The caravan trade was already well manned; there was no call now for a great influx of outsiders, such as there had been in the day when the Babylonian power promised a new development of northern Arabia. In the Roman time, all the world was open, and Arabia was perhaps the least promising of all accessible regions. There were in that day, moreover, historians who might well have preserved some record of any large Jewish migration southward; whereas in the neo-Babylonian time the history of Palestine is a blank. The supposition of the earlier date, which Müller finds difficult, really makes everything far more easily comprehensible. It is true, as he says, that these immigrants adopted the Arab ways of life and thought very thoroughly; but why he should suppose that in the course of additional centuries they would have been obliged to give up their religion and their "special peculiarities" is not clear. In the countries of Europe and other parts of the earth, even after very many centuries, these fundamental properties have been preserved, while in all else the native ways of life and thought have been adopted. We certainly have no reason to doubt that the professed Israelites of Teima, el-'Ōlā, Khaibar, Yathrib, Fadak, Mekka, and still other places, had been in these locations for a very long time.

The fact is, that outside the Koran we have very little trustworthy information in regard to the Israelites of northwestern Arabia. This is sufficiently demonstrated by D. S. Margoliouth in his brilliant little monograph (the Schweich Lectures for 1921) entitled *The Relations between Arabs and Israelites prior to the Rise of Islam.* He is principally concerned with the conditions in southern Arabia, but he also throws a well deserved dash of cold water on the theories of those who know too much about ethnic relations in the Hijaz. The epigraphic evidence from the south, which he and others discussed, will be found, however, to give us no real help.

The decipherment of the South Arabian inscriptions brought a new element into the discussion; how important an element, is not yet clear. It was well known that the Jews had played an important part in the history of Yemen shortly before the time of Mohammed. This meant certainly that they were very numerous; and probably, that they had been there long. It was natural to expect that some information in regard to them would be gained from this new epigraphic material. The problem of the Jews in the cities of the Hijaz was again brought forward. Might not the Judaism which inspired the Koran have come up from the south, rather than down from the north? A new and unexpected turn to the question came from one of these very cities of the Hijaz. Besides all the monuments—a veritable multitude—which were found in the extreme south of Arabia, there came to light in northern Arabia, between Khaibar and Teima, a series of inscriptions in the old South-Arabian characters. These are the so-called Liḥyānic inscriptions, all coming from the one place el-'Ölā, now identified with the Biblical Dedan.[6]

The date of these monuments is uncertain; the guesses range from 600 B.C. to the third or fourth century of the present era. It was a natural hope that they might contribute something toward the answer to our present problem, at least attesting the presence of Jews in the Hijaz. This possibility seemed to be brought nearer by the fact that the inscriptions employ a definite article ha, like the Hebrew—and, it should be added, like certain other dialects of the Semitic group. The search here for Hebrew names, or for definite indication of Israelite religious beliefs, has not been successful. In the main, the inscriptions are evidently pagan; and occasional features which might be interpreted as Jewish are really of too general a character to be used as evidence.

This little Himyarite settlement is an isolated phenomenon, and indeed remarkable. It is not at first obvious why a migration of city-dwellers from Yemen, who date their inscriptions by the regnal years of kings of Liḥyān, should have settled in this place, just south of Teima. I would hazard the conjecture that the same commercial opportunity, beginning in the sixth century B.C., which brought down colonists from the north also exercised its attraction in the south. El-'Ölā was a station of high importance in the caravan traffic through Arabia. Accepting the identification with Dedan, there are several Biblical passages which show that the place was well known to the Hebrews. In Is. 21:13 f. it is mentioned in connection with Teima. It was a frontier city, and apparently the northern limit ordinarily reached by the South Arabian carriers. "At el-'Ölā the Yemenite Arabs handed over their goods to the Nabataean Arabs, who took them to Teima. There the merchandise was divided: some went north; some was carried through Aila to Egypt; still other passed via Ha'il to Babylon" (O'Leary, 103 ff.). Here is obviously the best of reasons for a South Arabian colony in the north, and there seems

---

[6] [On this identification see Lidzbarski's *Ephemeris*, III, 273].

to be good reason for supposing that it was founded when, or soon after, Nabonidus took the step which meant so much to that region. But *these* immigrants, at all events, were not Israelites, nor do their inscriptions give any clear evidence of contact with them.

As for the 'Hebrew' definite article, it is also employed by those Bedouin tribes of South Arabia which migrated northward, as far as the upper Euphrates, at the beginning of the present era, scrawling their Thamudenic and Safatenic graffiti in debased Himyarite characters. There is no need to look for Hebrew influence in this grammatical feature, especially since the demonstrative element *ha* is so pervasive in all Semitic speech.

There remains, however, the fact of South Arabian Judaism, and the question of the extent to which it may have influenced the beginnings of Islam. The Koran contains some South Arabian material, as will appear; not, indeed, characteristically Jewish material. The real question concerns the main substance of Mohammedanism, not minor features. The large Israelite colonies in Mekka, Yathrib, Khaibar, and Teima were not themselves of Yemenite origin; this fact is clear and undisputed. But if, as many suppose, they were in culture and religion one-fourth Hebrew and three-fourths pagan; and if there is evidence that Judaism was, or had been, *the state religion* in one or more of the Yemenite kingdoms; then we might have some reason to believe that Mohammed's inspiration came, in some way, from the south. There are two questions here; and to the more important of the two, relating to the Jews of the Hijaz, I believe that a convincing answer can be given. The question of Jewish ascendancy in southern Arabia is more difficult.

It is well known that in the fifth and sixth centuries of the common era the Jews played an important rôle in Yemen. See, for example, the brief summary in Margolis and Marx, *History of the Jewish People*. They were at times influential politically, but by no means to an extent which would be likely to cause the spread of Judaism to other parts of the Arabian peninsula. On the contrary, Christian influence was paramount in Yemen during a part of this period. The only prospect of finding the prime source of Arabian Judaism in South Arabia therefore lay in the great collection of Himyaritic (Sabaean and Minaean) inscriptions already mentioned.

The subject is far too extensive to be entered upon here. These extremely important documents of an ancient high civilization, perhaps from 1000 B.C. onward, have been deciphered and elucidated by Halévy, Glaser, Mordtmann, D. H. Müller, and others; more recently especially by Rhodokanakis; and the question of a Hebrew element, both political and religious, has been eagerly discussed. It must suffice here to refer to the summary given by Margoliouth (*Arabs and Israelites,* pp. 59-70). He notes the presence, in a number of these inscriptions, of a monotheism which certainly may point ultimately to Hebrew influence, though he is inclined to think that it "developed out of paganism rather than out of Judaism" (p. 63). He remarks that "the supposed Judaism of the Himyari kings seems to elude the inquirer when he endeavours to lay hold on it" (p. 62). His final conclusion as to this matter is stated on p. 69: "It is clearly less certain than it used to be that Judaism ever held sway in any part of Arabia"; p. 81: "Supposing that a Jewish kingdom ever existed in South Arabia, it left little impression on the North Arabian mind"; and again, p. 70: "The origin of the Jewish communities of Yathrib or Medina must also remain in obscurity."

To some, perhaps to many, these conclusions will seem unduly skeptical. My own belief is, that as far as they concern the interpretation of the Himyaritic monuments they are fully justified; expressed, as they are, with caution. The problems of the northern settlements, however, are altogether different from those in the far south. In the latter case, the difficulty lies in the lack of evidence; in the former, the evidence is abundant, the difficulty is in the interpretation. The investigator is disappointed by the scarcity of Israelites in the one place, and scandalized by their apparent multitude in the other. In the absence of a plausible theory of extensive immigration, the hypothesis of converted Arab tribes seemed the only recourse.

Hugo Winckler, in his essay entitled "Arabisch-Semitisch-Orientalisch" published in the *Mitteilungen der Vorderasiatischen Gesellschaft* (1901, 4), pp. 1-223, was the first to say this emphatically. After remarking (72 f.)

that Wellhausen believed the "Beni Israel" of the Koran to be truly such in their racial origin, he replies, "Das ist unmöglich." We cannot suppose, he continues, that genuine Jews could have been in the Hijaz in such numbers. "Das Judentum, welches sich Arabien unterworfen hatte, ist durch die 'propaganda,' nicht durch Einwanderung oder gar Eroberung verbreitet worden." (The supposition of a Jewish military conquest of the Hijaz would indeed be amusing.) He concludes, that the wealthy "Israelite" tribes at Medina, as well as numerous others of which we hear, must have been coalitions of native clans induced by propaganda to profess Judaism.

Winckler's contention seemed indeed to be supported by what had been observed in the more favored parts of the ancient world. Eduard Meyer, *Ursprung und Anfänge des Christentums*, II, p. 353, would explain on a similar theory the great number of Jewish communities found not only in Western Asia but also in all the lands about the Mediterranean Sea, at the beginning of the present era and even earlier. Harnack, in his great work on the spread of Christianity (*Mission und Ausbreitung*, 4te Aufl., I, 12 f.), remarking that the Christian emissaries found the soil everywhere prepared for them by Judaism, explains the astonishing spread of the latter as mainly the result of successful proselyting. How otherwise account for the immense numbers which are so well attested? Georg Rosen, in his interesting little volume, *Juden und Phönizier* (1929), treats quite fully one principal phase of this theory. His son Friedrich, in a "Nachwort" to the volume, pp. 113 ff., quotes with good reason Wellhausen's remark (*Isr. u. jüd. Gesch.,*[5] p. 329), that the Jewish propaganda was a very different thing, in quality and lasting effect, from that of any other of the religions of the time; and also the saying of George Foot Moore (*Judaism*, I, 324), that Judaism was "the first great missionary religion of the Mediterranean world." The fact of very extensive and highly successful propaganda is indeed certain, though both its amount and its methods may have been somewhat overdrawn. The Hebrew Dispersion began considerably earlier and in greater volume than Meyer has supposed (*Ezra Studies*, 153, Note 23), while on the other hand Palestinian Jewry was constantly replenished from the surrounding lands. The remarkable fact remains, however; and when, for instance, the poet Horace alludes to the danger in Rome of forcible conversion to Judaism (*Sat.* I, 4, 142 f.), we know that behind the humorous exaggeration there was a background of popular gossip, which in turn had its origin in the knowledge of sudden and wholesale gains made by the Roman Jews.

Professor Margoliouth in his despair (as I should venture to term it) inclines to Winckler's view. The Jews of Yathrib, he remarks, have the Arab tribal organization. The names of the tribes are Arabic, and so, with few exceptions, are the names of the individual members of whom we happen to hear. We have no record of any outstanding Jewish antagonist of Mohammed; "neither do the supposed Jews of Medina appear to have produced any man whose name was worth preserving" (pp. 61, 70 f.). All this suggests, he would conclude, that the "children of Israel" whom Mohammed so constantly addresses were merely Arab tribes made Israelite by conversion—whatever that might mean.

Before weighing these arguments it is well to take into account the conditions in which the fruitful propaganda was undertaken, and the process by which great numbers were won over. The gain to be made, and the means of making it, were not the same in northern Arabia as in Egypt, Rome, and the highly civilized provinces of Asia and the Mediterranean shores. Moore's remark, quoted above, is elaborated by him (*ibid.*) as follows: "The Jews did not send out missionaries into the *partes infidelium* expressly to proselyte among the heathen. They were themselves settled by thousands in all the great centres and in innumerable smaller cities; they had appropriated the language and much of the civilization of their surroundings." Through all that early period the Jews were active in making proselytes, but in the main their influence was quietly pervasive. The successful appeal was made where their prosperity, their cohesion, and their superiority in culture, morals, and religion were manifest. *"They appropriated the language and much of the civilization of their surroundings."* The adoption of the native tribal organization, so fundamental to all Arabian life, would have been inevitable, even without the supposition of a long interval of time. The adoption of Gentile names is a very familiar fact in both ancient and modern times. And as for learned rabbis in Medina, could any one expect the traditions utilized by the first Muslim historians (who wrote long after Mohammed's day) to take notice of them? The Jewish tribe-names are like any other, though that of the Banu Zaghūra (Margoliouth, 60), obviously Aramaic, is worthy of notice. The name of the Banu Qainuqā' is descriptive of their occupations (smiths and armorers).

The superficial "conversion" of hordes of pagan Arabs by a few propagandists would appear, from the Jewish point of view, to be hardly worth the effort, even if we could make the thing seem plausible. From the standpoint of the Arabs themselves, what sufficient advantage can they possibly have seen in making profession of a religion about which (according to the hypothesis) they can have had little knowledge, and the results of which, in culture and morals, they cannot have seen exhibited in any decisive way? The hypothesis of propaganda really requires the presence in northwestern Arabia of genuine and large Jewish communities of long standing; that is, we are left with the problem still on our hands. The fact of the Israelite city of Khaibar, "the richest city of the Hijaz," is one very significant item among many. Such a civilization is not produced in a short time. Native Arab tribes "converted" in the manner supposed would have been certain, we should imagine, to welcome and accept the prophet of their own number who promised them a truly Arabian continuation of Judaism adapted to their own special needs, while based squarely on the Hebrew scriptures. But the Jews of Mekka, Medina, and the rest of the Hijaz knew better, and would not yield an inch.

I have thus far been speaking mainly of the *great number* of Arabs professing the Israelite faith, in Mohammed's time. Their *quality,* in civilization and religion, must also be considered. The weakest point in Professor Margoliouth's argument is his treatment, or lack of treatment, of *the Koran.* He descants (p. 71) on the woful ignorance which that book displays in regard to Hebrew matters in general, and attributes the ignorance to Mohammed's *soi-disant* Jewish mentors. But is it always the case that a great mass of strange and miscellaneous information is correctly reported by its recipient? We who are teachers by profession would hardly consent to be held responsible for everything which a half-trained pupil might hand out. There can be no question as to *Mohammed's* ignorance in many matters; but the amount of material, historical, folk-lorish, legislative, and religious, which he transmits with substantial correctness from purely Jewish sources is truly astonishing. This will appear plainly, I think, in the subsequent lectures. It is in great part material which he could only have obtained from learned men, well acquainted with the Hebrew sacred literature and the standard Jewish tradition. He revered, from the outset, both this great tradition and the people who embodied it—until his claim to be the world-prophet led to the clash which resulted in bitter enmity.

Margoliouth will have it that Mohammed had small respect for the Israelites of Mekka and Medina, saying (p. 81), "In relation to the native Arabs he thought of them as an inferior caste." I cannot imagine how this saying could be justified from the Koran, unless it means (as its context might possibly be held to imply) that the unbelieving Jews were destined for an especially deep-down compartment in the infernal regions. Of course all unbelievers stood on a lower plane than the Muslims. The Koran repeatedly speaks of "the children of Israel" as the most favored people on earth—up to the time of Islam; and in addressing them the prophet always reminds them that they know their scriptures. As has already been said with emphasis, he is not speaking of an imaginary people, but of his own neighbors. They were a people who in education and other inherited advantages stood higher than his own fellow-countrymen. *Tribes which were Jewish merely in name could not possibly have made any such impression on him.* As far as Mohammed and the Koran are concerned, the theory of Arab tribes superficially made Israelite by proselyting certainly breaks down completely, as an attempt to account for the origin of *the main body* of "the people of the Book" known to the prophet. Unquestionably some Arab tribes, as well as numerous smaller groups, had cast in their lot with the Israelites, in the centuries before Mohammed's day; gained over less through active propaganda than by the advantages which were silently offered. I shall show in a subsequent lecture that the Koran, in at least one place, takes account of certain of these brethren by adoption. They formed at all times a relatively small and unimportant element.

I have tried to sketch the theory of an ancient and extensive movement of colonization, a Hebrew migration southward into the Hijaz in the sixth century B.C., an ethnic transplanting which rooted deep and for many generations obeyed the injunction to be fruitful and multiply; and we may now return to it for a moment in closing. It implies a genuine Hebrew stock, and an authentic religious and literary tradition always kept alive and in continuous connection with the learned centers in the greater world outside Arabia. While presenting no historical difficulty, it can fully account for the relatively high civilization in the Jewish communities of Mekka, Yathrib, Teima, Khaibar, and other cities of that region.

It is a familiar fact that the Mishna takes account of Arabian Israelites. *Shabb.* 6, 6 notes that "the Arabian Jewesses go out wrapped in a veil, so that only their eyes are seen." *Ohaloth* 18, 10, speaking of the various places where dwellings in which pagans have lodged may be occupied by Jews without the contraction of ceremonial uncleanness, names "the tents of the Arabs." This is perfectly indefinite, to be sure, and each one of us is free to locate these particular Arabian Jews according to his own preference; still, the fact that they were numerous enough—and accessible enough—to be included in the Mishnic legislation is worthy of a thought in connection with the theory here advanced.

Among the early authorities cited in Talmud and Midrash is a certain Simeon the Teimanite (שמעון התימני). This, again, seems ambiguous inasmuch as the adjective could refer equally well either to the Edomite city (or district) Teimān or to Teimā. Since, however, the latter city is so well known as a strongly Jewish center even in pre-Mohammedan times, we may infer with confidence that it was the home [7] of this rabbi Simeon who was influential enough to be quoted as an authority. The passages are: *Mechilta* to 14, 15 (ed. Friedmann 29 b); Mishna *Yadayim* 1, 3; *Yebamoth* 4, 13 (an important passage); Tosephta *Berachoth* 4, 24 (p. 10); *Sanhedr.* 12, 3; *Besa* 2, 19; Bab. Talmud *Zebachim* 32 b; *Baba*

---

[7] [According to *Sanhedr.* 17 b he was in Yabneh in the time of Rabbi Aqiba].

Qamma 90 b; *Besa* 21 a.[8] Margoliouth, *Relations,* 58 f., takes notice of the Arabic words occurring in the early Jewish tradition, including the Mishna, and names a number of them, but remarks in conclusion: "On the whole, however, it is surprising how rarely the rich language of the Mishna and its copious technicalities of agriculture and commerce can be satisfactorily illustrated from Arabic." Might not one rather say, that it is noteworthy that this rich language should draw at all upon the Arabic in the terminology of agriculture(!) or even of commerce? And when, in the formula for a bill of divorce given in *Gittin* 85 b, ואגרת שבוקין וגט פטורין (!) ספר תרוכין, the first of the three terms is Arabic, the plain evidence of communities of Arabic-speaking Jews is striking and important.

Far more important, however, is the testimony contained in the Koran. The Israelite tribes with their rabbis, their books, sacred and secular, their community of faith and action, and their living contact with the past, are there; they are no phantom. All through the Koran there is evidence of a Jewish culture, which Mohammed greatly admired, and of Jewish learning, which he very imperfectly assimilated. Of this culture, and of Mohammed's attempt to digest the learning, the subsequent lectures will try to take account.

[8] [I owe these references to the kindness of Professor Spiegel, of the Jewish Institute of Religion].

THE GENESIS OF THE NEW FAITH

The word "culture," in its ordinary English meaning, is perhaps not often employed in speaking of the pre-Mohammedan tribesmen of northern and western Arabia. Their life is typical of something more interesting. There are certain groups of men, and phases of primitive civilization, the mention of which always creates a picture of hardship and valor, the triumph of human skill and endurance over natural conditions full of danger and privation. We find a flavor more appetizing than the taste of high life in Cooper's novels, and in the biographies of Daniel Boone and Kit Carson. When we read of the typical "cowboys" of a generation ago, we expect no mention of books and reading, of household luxuries and bric-a-brac; what we seek, and find, in the story of their life on the plains is a picture more entertaining, and also far more truly representative of their civilization—or lack of it.

It is this appeal to the imagination which is made by the native of Arabia, in whatever variety of literature he is depicted. We see proud tribes, and their noted heroes, restlessly moving figures in a most forbidding landscape. We think of the exploits of Antar; the savage deeds of the freebooter and poet Shanfarā, with every man's hand against him; Ta'abbata-sharran following the trail through the desert; the tent-dweller kindling for a passing stranger his hoarded pile of brushwood, and sharing with him the last handful of dates—nay, giving him the whole of it. The narratives in that great storehouse, the Aghani; the poems of the earliest period; and the quasi-historical works whose material is chiefly

derived from these two sources; all give this lively picture of the Arabia
of Mohammed's day and earlier. They are concerned with the heroic and
the picturesque, and hold in some contempt the humdrum ease of the
town dwellers. Listen to al-Quṭāmī, of the tribe of Taghlib (Nöldeke,
Del. Carm. Arab., 31):

> You, who admire the life of the city dwellers,
>> What think you of us, the sons of the open desert?
> You may jog the streets on asses; we have our chargers,
>> Clean-limbed, and our lances, strong and keen for plunder.
> When times are straitened, we raid the clans of Ḍabba;
>> Then he whose time has come to die—he dies!
> Ay, it may happen to us to raid our brethren,
>> When for our need no other foe comes handy.

They take justifiable pride in the strenuous life of their ancestors, so
largely deprived of the comforts and even decencies of civilization; while
of course knowing that there is another side to the picture. There is a
popular saying which holds up to view one less desirable feature of life
in the desert: "Everything is soap for the Bedouin." [9] Doubtless; but those
who coined the proverb knew the virtues of this toilet article, and presumably used it. The luxuries of the desert are the necessities of the city.
All the time, as far back as any of our sources reach, the city life is there,
even when little or nothing is said about it.

We are gradually learning, in these days, that the ancient races in the
Orient were much farther advanced in their knowledge of arts and
crafts, and in their general culture, than we had supposed. The low estimate was a matter of course, while the evidence of high attainment was
lacking. Even in the case of unpromising Arabia, I have no doubt that
our estimate has been too low. Note, for example, the evidence collected
by Wellhausen, *Reste*, 201, note 2, in regard to the *written* tradition of the
old Arabian poetry. There may have been much more writing of both
poetry and prose than we have been wont to imagine. We are aware

[9] [Landberg, *Proverbes et Dictons du Peuple Arabe*, p. 170].

that the cities of South Arabia were magnificent and their culture well advanced, though our knowledge of them is still meager. Our definite information in regard to the cities in the northwestern part of the peninsula is very slight indeed, but even here we have ground for a probable conclusion.

The caravan trade did little for the Bedouins; they continued to live as they always had lived; but it did much for the emporia along the route. The products and symbols of a high civilization, in great number and variety, had for many centuries been familiar to the merchants and townspeople of the Hijaz. The influence of such acquaintance, long continued, is inevitably profound. As for Mekka, aside from the "through" traffic in which their participation was but slight, there were the local "caravans of winter and summer" mentioned by Mohammed in Sura 106; the caravan of winter going down to Yemen, and that of summer to the cities of Palestine, Syria, and Phoenicia. Mekka even had some importance as a junction, from which a trade route ran by way of Riad to Gerrha on the Persian Gulf. These merchants carried exports, and brought back imports. They also brought a change in modes of thought and habits of life, a wider horizon. How much of a gulf there was between the civilization of the roving clans of Suleim or Hudheil and that of the Qoreish of Mekka, we are not in a position to say; but a gulf there certainly was.

The Koran, in that portion of it which was composed at Mekka, gives the impression of a community both prosperous and enlightened. Those citizens (not named) who are attacked by the prophet as troublesome opponents are not merely wealthy and influential, there were among them men for whose knowledge and wider experience he had a wholesome respect. This means not only the Jews; though in knowledge of books and of religious history their communities certainly were no slight distance in advance of their Arab neighbors.

In such centers of an old civilization as Mekka, Yathrib, Khaibar, and Teima the ability to read and write had for centuries, as a matter of course, gone far beyond the requirement of mercantile transactions. The acquisition of these accomplishments was very easy, and the advantage derived from them very obvious. Schools of some sort must have been ancient institutions in the Hijaz, even though we know nothing in regard to them. Our sources give us no sure ground for conjecture as to the proportion of illiteracy in Mekka and Medina, nor as to the attainments of Mohammed's companions in general. There is a tradition, not given in Ibn Hishām's Life of the Prophet, but quite credible as to the main fact, to the effect that in the second year of the Hijra, after the battle of Bedr, some of the Mekkan captives were made to serve as schoolmasters, to teach the Muslim boys. This has sometimes been too hastily interpreted to mean that the Muslims themselves were for the most part illiterate. The implication is not necessary, however. We at the present day hire teachers for our children, not because we are unable to read and write, but because we are busy. Those who had migrated from Mekka with Mohammed were now reduced to dire straits in order to earn their living. They could not long remain as parasites on the so-called "Helpers" of Medina who had given them hospitality, but must shift for themselves in every possible way. Doubtless many, both of the emigrants and of the Helpers, were illiterate; but we can hardly doubt that the men of the better class had had the benefit of some schooling. We happen to know that this was true even of some of the slaves. Mohammed's legislation in Sura 24:33 implies that written contracts were a matter of course, and that his followers would have no difficulty in making them.

In regard to the Jews of either city we have better ground for an estimate. They were an educated people. If, as the available evidence makes probable, their settlements in this part of Arabia were ancient and chiefly the result of a considerable migratory movement, we could take it for granted that they brought with them and maintained the traditions of culture which they carried forth and perpetuated in other parts of the world. Their worship required a succession of learned men, and their laws necessitated a general religious training. The Arab tales and traditions, in their mention of the Israelites of the Hijaz, give everywhere the impression of a people relatively high in civilization. The respect with which Mohammed, even in his utmost exasperation, speaks of this "people of the Book" shows that for him they stood on a superior plane; and this not merely because of their religious inheritance, but also because they possessed knowledge of history and literature to an extent which differentiated them, as a people, from any native Arab community. It is not merely a few men that he has in mind; the manner in which he speaks of "the children of Israel" shows that his thought is of the Jewish people in general, as he and his fellows had come in contact with them. In our conception of the state of civilization represented by them we probably shall underestimate rather than the contrary.

What literature may we suppose the Jews of the Hijaz to have possessed, in the time of Mohammed? On the theory of their origin here presented —the only possible theory, I maintain, to account for the plain facts before us—the question can be answered with very high probability. If these Hebrew settlements had existed since the sixth century B.C., and had kept in touch with the outside world (as they could not have failed to do, in view of the constant and very lively traffic), their history in this respect was like that of other Jewish colonies. Certainly they had all the *sacred* literature possessed by their neighbors in Palestine and Babylonia. They were indeed in a part of the world utterly different from any of the regions occupied by their brethren of the Dispersion. Life in Arabia had its unavoidable requirements, and they had become Arab tribesmen, at least externally; but they kept their religion, and their traditions; it is hardly conceivable that they should have done otherwise. Religious feeling, long-established customs, pride of race, consciousness of the great superiority of the Israelite faith to the native paganism, the influence of frequent visitors from the Jewish communities in the north and east, the enduring reputation of such learned Arabian Jews as Simeon of Teima and doubtless others whose names we do not know—these factors, especially, were potent in maintaining Arabian Judaism. Obvious and acknowledged superiority is not readily thrown away. It would have been easier to forsake the faith and the inherited practices in Rome or Alexandria than in the oases of the desert. The colonists, here as elsewhere, brought with them their sacred books, and scribes were of course raised up as they were needed.

Outside the Koran we should hardly expect to find any contemporary

allusion to the *learning* of these Israelites. We do know that two of the
large Jewish tribes of Medina, the Naḍīr and the Quraiẓa, were called
the *Kāhinānī* (i. e. the two *ḳāhin* tribes); the name indicating that they
claimed, doubtless with good reason, that their membership included certain priestly families.[10] In Ibn Hishām's Life of the Prophet (ed. Wüsten-
feld, p. 659) there is preserved a poem by a Jewish contemporary of Mohammed which deserves attention. It dates from the third year of the
Hijra, when Muslims and Jews were already in open hostility. One of
the latter, Ka'b ibn al-Ashraf, who was connected with the tribe Naḍīr,
had made himself especially obnoxious to the prophet, and was accordingly
assassinated, by high command. A well known Muslim poet, Ka'b ibn
Mālik, composed verses justifying the murder, blaming the Jews for their
failure to support the true prophet, the heaven-sent messenger. A formal
reply, as usual in the same rhyme and meter, was returned by Sammāk of
Naḍīr, and in it occur the following lines:

　　arā 'l-ahbāra tunḳiruhū jamī'an
　　　　we-ḳulluhum lahū 'ilmun ḳhabīrū
　　we-ḳānū 'd-dārisīna liḳulli 'ilmin
　　　　bihī 't-taurātu tanṭiqu wa-'z-zubūrū

The doctors all, I note, refuse him credence,
　　All of them learned, men of worldly wisdom;
They who are versed in all the heavenly teaching
　　Uttered for us in Torah and in Psalter.

The verses are unquestionably authentic, and in view of the circumstances
under which they were uttered we can be quite certain that no one in
Medina at that time would have denied the claim which they make. In
the Israelite tribes of the city there were men whose reputation for learning was generally known. The verses are also interesting for their Hebrew
loanwords, four in number; reminding of August Müller's remark

10 [See Nöldeke, *Beiträge zur Kenntniss der Poesie der alten Araber*, p. 54 f.; also Margoliouth, *Relations*, 73, 79].

(quoted above, p. 17) in regard to the "Jewish Arabic" spoken by the
Israelites of the Hijaz. These same words appear frequently in the Koran,
and it is evident that the most of the terms of this nature which Mohammed employs had been in common use long before his time.[11]

The Koran occasionally—and, be it noted, also in the Mekkan period—
takes notice of the Jewish scholars (*aḥbār*),[12] the rabbis (*rabbānīs*), the
word denoting a still more learned class (Geiger, p. 52), as in 3:73 and
5:48, 68. In 26:197 Mohammed boasts that "the learned (*ulemā'*) of the
children of Israel" had given him encouragement. This incidental testimony, supported as it is by the whole Koran, is certainly to be taken at its
face value. To assert that there *were* no Israelite scholars in Mekka and
Medina, and that Mohammed did not know the difference between the
learned and the unlearned, is easy, but quite in disregard of the evidence.
All the history of his dealing with "the people of the Book"—the amount
of exact information, from Biblical and rabbinical sources, which he received; the encouragement given him while he seemed a harmless inquirer; the long and bitter argument, in which he was continually worsted;
and the final rejection of all his prophetic claims—shows him in close contact with an old and perfectly assured religious tradition, far too strong
for him. The history would have been the same if he had made his appearance, first as pupil and then as dangerous innovator, in any center of
Israelite culture.

The sacred books were there, in Mekka, and Mohammed had seen some
of them—though he takes care not to say so. It is altogether probable,
moreover, that each of the principal Jewish communities in the Hijaz
possessed considerable collections of volumes—scrolls and codices; not
only the Torah, the Prophets, and other books of the Bible; not merely
also the authoritative rabbinical writings, as they successively appeared;

---

[11] [The Hebrew terms רבח, שׁרד הרות in the quoted verses are obvious enough. *Zubūr*
comes from רומזמ under the influence of a genuine Arabic root *zbr*, "writing"; an especially
good example of this Hijāzī dialect. It is unnecessary to argue that the Jews of Mekka and
Medina did not adopt this word from Mohammed (!); and he, for his part, was not so
simple as to invent Hebrew technical terms in place of those already in use].

[12] [Rudolph, *Abhängigkeit*, 5, note 31, is mistaken in supposing that in Sura 9:31, 34
Mohammed designates *Christian* scholars by this word. The context plainly shows the con-
trary].

but also the most important and most widely diffused works of the world-literature, including translations from such languages as the Syriac and Ethiopic. Libraries grow up slowly; but even a small nucleus is a very strong magnet, and the man who loves books will collect them, when, as in the present case, they are within easy reach. The Jews, by long tradition, were a people of books and reading; and wherever their culture struck deep root, some sort of literary activity was a matter of course. In the generations immediately succeeding the destruction of the temple at Jerusalem by the Romans they clung closely to their canonical books and their religious tradition, letting everything else go by the board. This was partly the result of the calamities which had overtaken them, looked upon as a severe lesson, and partly in opposition to the Christian literature which was growing up, professedly based on the Hebrew and Jewish scriptures, canonical and extra-canonical.

This attitude underwent a gradual change, of necessity, and that not only in the lands of the Dispersion. Before the time of Mohammed the haggadic midrash was gathering and adapting material from the Gentile literature, generally giving it a new religious coloring. The legends regarding Alexander the Great afford an interesting example. Any parenetic narrative, pagan or Christian, might be laid under contribution, for no religion can build a fence around a good story. In a subsequent lecture, dealing with the narratives of the Koran, attention will be called to a remarkable series of legends in the 18th Sura, all belonging to the West Asiatic folklore. The collection was not made by Mohammed; the stories were merely abridged and adapted by him in characteristic fashion. It has been observed that a very considerable portion of these same legends is to be found in the homilies of Jacob of Sarug, a Mesopotamian Christian who wrote at the end of the fifth century; see especially the first chapter in Huber, *Die Wanderlegende von den Siebenschläfern*. The first in the Koranic series is a Christian tale, that of the Seven Sleepers of Ephesus. Every Christian element has been removed from it, however, and it would serve equally well as a story of Israelites persecuted for their faith. There is even some evidence that the Jews of Mekka regarded the legend as their own property, and quizzed Mohammed in regard to it (Nöldeke-Schwally,

139–143). Next comes a parable which, as many scholars have observed, sounds like a typical Hebrew *mashal*. Thereupon follow old pagan legends in a Jewish redaction, Moses taking the place, first, of Alexander the Great, then of the old Babylonian hero Gilgamesh (see the Fourth Lecture). It is perfectly evident that Mohammed's source was an already fixed collection of Jewish tales, existing at Mekka, in whatever manner he may have received them.

This I should suppose to be typical of a class of literature, designed for popular instruction, which might be found in any or all of the Israelite settlements, from Teima to Mekka. That it was in the Aramaic language, and written with the Aramaic alphabet, would be a matter of course; some direct evidence touching this question will be noticed presently. It is unlikely that any portion of this "world-literature" existed in the Arabic language in the time of Mohammed. The interesting narratives might be well known, however, even if they were not obtained from the Jews. The Arabs of Hira were bilingual, and so also, no doubt, were many of those on the Greek frontier; and the art of the story-teller flourished mightily in Arabia. But in the case just mentioned we certainly are dealing with *a document,* not with oral tradition.

Could Mohammed read and write? This may seem a very strange question, in the presence of the Koran. Would not the production, by an illiterate man, of a great literary work, admirable throughout in its discriminating use of words, the skilful structure of its sentences, and the surprising mastery of all the *nuances* of a very highly developed grammatical science, be in fact the miracle which it claims to be? The answer, however, is not such a matter of course as it seems. The grammar, i. e. the forms of the literary language, had long been completely developed in the pre-Mohammedan poems, which were a multitude and familiar throughout the Arabian peninsula; and oral tradition can accomplish wonders. It is with the Arabic language only that the question is ordinarily concerned; but if it should be answered in the affirmative, it is necessary to go farther, and inquire whether there is any likelihood that the prophet could also read Hebrew or Aramaic. This might at the outset seem very improbable indeed, but there are no known facts which could warrant the assertion that it is impossible.

The direct evidence, it is needless to say, is scanty and difficult of interpretation. The orthodox Muslim Tradition generally (but not quite consistently) maintains that the prophet could neither read nor write. It is quite evident that dogmatic considerations were chiefly influential here. We have to reckon with a tendency, not simply with a record of known facts. As for the testimony of the Koran, it can be, and has been, interpreted in more than one way. It is quite natural that the prophet should not take occasion to affirm his ability, if he possessed it. The real question is whether he does not *deny* the ability. Some have claimed in support of this view the passage 29:47, in which the angel of revelation says to Mohammed, "You have not been wont to recite any (sacred) scripture before this, nor to transcribe it with your right hand; otherwise those who set it at nought might well have doubted." But this is a very dubious argument, to say the least. As Nöldeke-Schwally, 14, remarks, it can be turned the other way. The natural implication of the passage is that the prophet was writing down the Suras of this particular "Book," though he never before had undertaken any such portentous task (cf. also 87:6). And I believe that it will be found probable, when all the evidence is taken into account, that Mohammed did write down the whole of the Koran 'with his right hand.' This passage will come under consideration again, in the sequel.

The argument which has weighed heaviest with those who would have Mohammed illiterate is the fact that he repeatedly describes himself as "*ummī*," a curious Koranic adjective which always expresses contrast with the "people of the Book." Interpreting this as "unlettered," and supporting the interpretation by the Tradition and the prevailing low estimate of Arabian culture, Nöldeke in his *Geschichte des Qorāns* (1860) adjudged Mohammed illiterate, or nearly so. Wellhausen adopted this view, expressing it with emphasis, and it was generally accepted; Sprenger (*Das Leben und die Lehre des Mohammad,* 1861–1865) was one of a few who maintained the opposite. More recently, there has been a growing tendency to predicate for the prophet some literary training; thus Grimme, Rudolph, Schulthess, and others. In Nöldeke-Schwally, 14, it is shown that *ummī* cannot mean "illiterate"; and the view there maintained is that it designated those who do not have ("or know") the ancient holy scriptures. Even this explanation, however, is unsatisfactory. It does not at all account for the statement in 2:73 (see below); nor does it provide a reasonable derivation of the strange adjective, which certainly cannot be explained by *'am ha-areṣ* (!), nor by any native Arabic use of *umma*, "nation." On the contrary, this is one of the Jewish-Arabic locutions of which August Müller speaks, being simply the transfer into Arabic of the Hebrew *gōi, gōyīm*. It was not coined by Mohammed, but was taken over by him from the speech which he heard. It designated any and all *who were not of the Israelite race* (as has already been said, and is well known, Mohammed does not distinguish Christians from Israelites). The passage 2:73, which has made trouble for previous explanations of the problematic term, expresses the indignation and scorn with which the prophet replies to certain *proselytes* in one of the Medinese tribes, who had tried to trick or ridicule him by means of some "scripture" of their own composition— a most natural proceeding for would-be Israelites. He has just been speaking of the Jews, and now continues: "And among them there are certain *goyīm,* who do not know the scriptures, but only hope to appear to, and who think vain things. Woe to those who write out scriptures with their hands and then say, This is from God!" Here, the adjective is plainly used in reproach and contempt; elsewhere, it means precisely "Gentile," most obviously in 3:69! The Koran, then, gives no ground whatever for supposing Mohammed unlettered.

On one point, at all events, there has been very general agreement among students of the Koran, namely, that Mohammed did not wish to seem to be one to whom reading and writing were familiar accomplishments. This, however, is a little too sweeping a statement of the case. He did not wish to seem to be a man of book-learning; to be dealing out what had been obtained from writings. He had not copied books, nor parts of books, nor written down what any man had dictated. The reason for this is obvious: he would not weaken the assurance, constantly main-

tained, that his outgivings were of superhuman origin. God was now producing and perfecting for the Arabs *a holy book,* delivered through his
Arabian messenger in the same way in which the Jews and Christians
had received their scriptures. The prophets of Israel had spoken by divine
inspiration, not from book-knowledge. Mohammed himself certainly never
doubted, from the beginning of his ministry to the day of his death, that
his 'Koran' was the product of divine illumination, nor would he have
others doubt. We are reminded of one of the great teachers of the New
Testament. The apostle Paul had read Christian gospels, and had talked
with disciples and companions of Jesus; but neither in his own thought
nor in his writings would he allow these facts any weight. The truth was
revealed to him, he repeatedly declares; "I conferred not with flesh and
blood"; "They who were of repute imparted nothing to me" (Gal. 1:16;
2:6). Mohammed would have used the same words: the Koran came to
him from above, not from any human teachers, nor from the reading of
books.

This is very different from a profession of unfamiliarity with reading
and writing, nor is it easy to believe that he could have made any such
profession. When we think of the period of preparation—certainly not a
brief period—which preceded the beginning of the Koran and the public
appearance of the prophet, it seems truly incredible that he should not
have made himself familiar with these very ordinary accomplishments. It
is altogether likely, indeed, that he had possessed them from his boyhood.
The family of Hāshim, to which he belonged, was respected in Mekka,
though neither wealthy nor especially influential. His grandfather 'Abd al-
Muṭṭalib and his uncle Abu Ṭālib, in whose care he was brought up,
mighᵗ certainly have been expected to give him some of the education
which Mekkan boys of good family were wont to enjoy. The fact that he
was chosen by the prosperous widow Khadīja (whom he afterwards married) as the man to take charge of her trading ventures would seem to
make it almost certain that he was known to have some acquaintance with
"the three Rs."

Supposing that all this is granted, the probability that Mohammed had
learned to read Hebrew or Aramaic in any effective way may nevertheless

seem remote. Not that the acquisition would have been difficult, a short
time would have sufficed; but because he could get what he wanted in a
much quicker and easier way. The alphabet could indeed be mastered in
a few hours; and the two languages, in both vocabulary and grammar,
bear enough resemblance to the Arabic to enable one who is accustomed
to read and write the latter to labor through the sentences of a Jewish
document after a comparatively short period of study with the aid of a
Jewish instructor. In view of Mohammed's great interest in the Jewish
scriptures, and the length of time during which he must have been receiving instruction in them; in view also of certain features in the Koran,
it is easy to believe that he may have gained this gentle eminence in comparative Semitic philology. It is perhaps not too fanciful a conjecture that
the brief exclamatory utterance which is believed with good reason to
have constituted the very beginning of the Koran contains reference to
this fact. Sura 96, 3–5: "Recite! for thy Lord is the most gracious One;
who teaches the use of the pen; teaches man what he had not known."
The three lines are built upon the word *qalam,* "pen," which furnishes
the threefold rhyme. Doubtless the thought of the Jewish and Christian
scriptures is in the background; but we should hardly expect the human
element in the divine revelation to be so strongly emphasized, in this brief
outburst, unless the message to the Arabs was also in mind. There is a
personal note in the announcement: *"Thy* Lord is most gracious." It is
natural to think that the nascent prophet here speaks out of the consciousness of his own experience.

However this may be, no wielding of the *qalam,* nor ability to spell out
the words of an ancient sacred book, can account for Mohammed's acquaintance with Hebrew and Jewish lore. It is quite evident from the
volume and variety of the material, derived from literary sources, which
the Koran brings before us that it cannot, in the main, have been derived
from the prophet's own reading. It would indeed have been easy for
him to peruse, with the help of a teacher, some portions of the Hebrew
sacred writings; it seems the easiest explanation of some of the phenomena
which we can observe in the Koran that he did this; but, even if this may
be supposed, the amount of such laborious perusal must have been small

at best. The manner in which he gained his extensive, even though superficial acquaintance with the Hebrew scriptures and the Jewish halakha and haggada was by oral instruction, teaching which must have covered a very considerable period of time.

We have no definite and trustworthy information either as to the place, or places, where the instruction was given, or as to any individual who gave it (see, however, what is presently to be said in regard to the passage 16:105). Presumably the prophet's own city, Mekka, was the principal place, and perhaps it was the only one, during his preliminary training and the earlier part of his career. It has often been surmised, and sometimes treated as an assured fact, that Mohammed gained some, or much, of his religious information abroad, while on his travels as a caravan master, especially in Syria. The conjecture, however, is neither well founded nor helpful. There is in the Koran nothing whatever that could not easily have been obtained in Mekka and Medina, nor any sort of material for which an origin outside of Arabia seems likely. The stories of Mohammed's distant journeyings are purely fanciful; it is not likely that he ever went north of Teima, the distributing center where the caravan merchandise was taken over by the carriers to the north and east. Nothing in the Koran gives the suggestion of a man who had been abroad; one receives distinctly the contrary impression.

The number of the prophet's authorities must have been small. It is possible to assert this from our knowledge of the man himself. He was not one who could go about freely and openly, asking for information— even before the idea of an Arabian revelation first entered his head; nor was it ever characteristic of him to take others into his confidence. In the *hadīth* there are some very circumstantial narratives which show that on occasions when Mohammed was in serious need of counsel, even Omar and the trusted companion and adviser Abu Bekr were held off at arm's length.[13] We should have known this from the Koran, without the aid of the *hadīth*. He was not a man to make intimate friends; if he had been, he never would have stepped forth as a prophet. He consulted pri-

[13] [E. g. Bokhari, ed. Krehl, II, 105, 156].

vately as few as possible of those who could give him what he wanted, and kept his own counsel. Knowing how he was wont to treat—and maltreat —his material, we can say without reserve that he was very fortunate in the choice of his teachers. He can hardly have discussed with them much of what they told him. If he had done so, he certainly would have been saved from many of the blunders into which he fell. It would seem probable, from what we know of the mental attitude of the man, revealed in every feature of his life and work, that even in the presence of learned men he did not wish to acknowledge to them, or to himself, that he was acquiring information which was totally new. Whatever he thus received was a divine gift, to be refashioned according to his own divinely aided wisdom. This conception of the matter would have been especially easy if (as we may suppose) he had already learned to spell out Hebrew words and decipher sentences for himself. Probably few of his contemporaries, aside from the teachers themselves, knew whom he had been consulting; and certainly no one of the latter, not knowing what other instructors Mohammed might have had, would be inclined to accept responsibility for the travesty of Hebrew history which the Arabian prophet put forth. He had not been given this history in connected form, but in fragments of narrative, largely unrelated—and he trusted Gabriel to put them together for him.

His studies certainly attracted very little attention at the time. In his youth and early manhood, and until his public appearance as a prophet, he was an insignificant personage, not particularly noticed by anybody (see Snouck Hurgronje, *op. cit.,* 657). Mekkan tradition preserved no record of his teacher or teachers. The legends of the monk Bahira, of his Ten Jewish Companions, etc., are all perfectly worthless, mere romancing. His "studies" were indeed observed and commented upon. In two very important passages the Koran refers to human instruction received by the prophet, in both cases in answer to the cavilling charge that his divine wisdom was only what might be acquired by any one who was willing to waste his time in listening to "old stories." The first of the passages is 25:5 f. "The unbelievers say: This is only falsehood of his own devising, and other people have helped him to it. . . . . And they say: Old stories, which he has written out for himself; and they are dictated to him morning and evening." This is instruction *given in Mekka,* extending over some time. The stories from the Old Testament are especially referred to. Mohammed does not deny the human teacher, but only insists that the teaching came down from heaven. What the scoffing Mekkans said was certainly true as to the process by which the narrative material in the Koran was generally obtained. The teacher was some one whose continued intercourse with Mohammed they could observe, there in their own city. It was at home, not abroad, that the prophet received at least the Biblical (and haggadic) narratives which occupy so large a part of the Koran. The word *qaum,* "people," in this passage is indeed quite indefinite; it need not imply more than a single instructor. Since, however, the material referred to is Jewish, and since also we know that during nearly the whole of the Mekkan period it was upon the Jews and their knowledge of holy writ that he relied, it is a fair inference that the reference is to a representative of this "people," the Israelite colony in Mekka.

A still more important passage, significant in more ways than one, is 16:105, also of Mekkan origin. The angel of revelation is the speaker. "We know very well that they say: It is only a mortal man who has taught him. *But the language of him to whom they refer is foreign,* while *this* language is clear Arabic!" The person here referred to may or may not be the same one who is mentioned in 25:5. Certainly nothing opposes the supposition that both passages point to the same individual, while it is clearly supported by two considerations especially: these portions of the Koran are of about the same date; and Mohammed never would have frequented two or more teachers if one would suffice. It plainly is implied here that the Mekkans knew of but one, namely *"that one whom they have in mind."* Here, then, we may fairly conclude, is Mohammed's chief source, very likely his only major source of instruction aside from what he was constantly seeing and hearing, in the Jewish community which he frequented.

Especially interesting is the statement regarding the language. The man was a Jew; additional reason for this statement will be given in the sequel. He was not of Arabian birth, but came from without. As already remarked, the old and highly prosperous Israelite colonies in the Hijaz were frequently enlarged, both from Arabia and from the outside world. On the one hand, they inevitably attracted considerable companies of proselytes. Whole Arab tribes or clans would be likely to join them, assimilating more or less completely their religion and culture.[14] Small groups of foreigners arriving in the country would see their best prospect of protection and success in entering the strong Hebrew settlements and professing the Israelite faith. I have shown reason for believing that we have in 2:73 a highly interesting allusion to certain of these "Israelites for revenue only." (page 38). In the first lecture, moreover (p. 15), I spoke of Jews who came from foreign parts to join their co-religionists in the Hijaz. One of these was the man to whom the prophet is now alluding. This learned rabbi (for such he certainly was), resident in Mekka among those of his own race and presumably speaking their dialect, had not been in Arabia long enough to enable him to speak Arabic correctly. Any discourse uttered, or dictation provided, by him would at once have been recognized as 'ajamī (the word employed in the passage just translated). The word most commonly, but not necessarily, points to the Persian domain, and on all accounts it seems the most probable conjecture that this was a Babylonian Jew who had come down with one of the caravans from the northeast. (It seems characteristic of Mohammed to resort to such an outsider, for his private tutoring, rather than to any of those with whom the Arabs of Mekka were well acquainted.) There are some features of the Koranic diction, especially in the proper names, which suggest a teacher who was accustomed to Syriac forms; [15] and a portion of the material taken over by Mohammed, especially the legends in the 18th Sura (mentioned above; and see especially the Fourth Lecture) and the quite unusual bit of mythology introducing the Babylonian angels Hārūt and Mārūt (Sura 2:96) [16] would naturally point the reader to southern Mesopotamia.

---

[14] [See Nöldeke, *Beiträge zur Kenntniss der Poesie der alten Araber*, p. 55].

[15] [The name Yājūj was probably adapted by the Arabs—Jewish and Christian—of southern 'Irāq from the "Agōg" which appears in the Syriac legend of Alexander].

[16] [See Littmann, in the Andreas *Festschrift*, 70–87, and Horovitz, *Kor. Untersuchungen*, 146 ff.].

Whether Mohammed had only one habitual instructor in Mekka, or more than one, he certainly learned from many, and in many ways. The essential framework of the new faith he had built up from his own observation and deep meditation, without consulting anybody. By far the most important factor in his religious education was the close and long continued acquaintance with the actual practice of a superior religion. He had frequented the Jewish quarter in his native city until he had learned much in regard to the children of Israel, "whom Allah preferred over the rest of the world" (45:15, and elsewhere): their fundamental beliefs, their book-learning, their forms of worship, and some of the laws and customs which regulated their private and social life. Without this personal experience, seeing the actual example with his own eyes and observing it for a considerable time, he could not possibly have conceived Islam.

Doubtless regarded as a promising convert, he was permitted to see the sacred books and to witness the divine service. The impression made upon him was profound. There is a very significant passage in the third Sura which has not received due attention. In verses 106–110 the prophet contrasts the Muslims with the unbelievers among the Jews, while acknowledging that some of the latter are true believers. In the past, as he has often declared, the children of Israel were the preferred of Allah, but this is true no longer. (106) "You (the Muslims) are the best people that has been brought forth for mankind; . . . . if the people of the Book had believed, it would have been better for them. *There are believers among them,* but the most of them are perverse. (107) They can do you little harm; and if they do battle against you, they will turn their backs in flight. (108) Shame is decreed for them, ... and they have incurred the wrath of God; and poverty is stamped upon them; this, because they denied the signs of God, and slew the prophets unjustly (repeating the list of charges and penalties given in 2:58, 84 f.). (109) Yet all are not alike: among the people of the book is an upright folk, *reciting the signs of God in the night season, and prostrating themselves."* Rudolph, p. 8, strangely holds, against the whole context, that this last verse may refer to the Christians; apparently unaware that the Jews, as well as the Christians, kept vigils and prayed with genuflections and prostrations.

Certainly Mohammed had witnessed nocturnal Jewish devotions, both the prayer ritual and the recitation (chanting) of the Hebrew scriptures. From the former he devised his own prescription of a prayer season in the night (11:116; 17: 80 f.; 76: 25 f.; and see p. 136); while it was in partial imitation of the latter that he devised the form of his *Qur'ān,* with its rhythmic swing and—especially—the clearly marked-off verses (*āyāt,* "signs."). It was in order to assert the originality of his own "recitation," moreover, in distinction from that of the Jews, that he uttered the words of 29:47: "You (Mohammed) have not been wont to recite any scripture before this, nor to transcribe it with your right hand." He had neither recited Jewish scriptures nor copied them—a charge which would inevitably have been made by the Mekkans.

It is perhaps useless to conjecture what writings other than the Hebrew scriptures, specimens of the widespread Aramaic literature, might have been shown to him and perhaps read by him, at least in part. One might think of Bible stories in popular form, or of other religious narratives. In spite of the very strong probability that the most of what he received was given to him orally, and chiefly on the basis of oral tradition, there is a certain amount of literary transmission to be taken into account. I may be permitted to refer to a conjecture of my own, published in *A Volume of Oriental Studies presented to Edward G. Browne* (1922), pp. 457 ff. The story of the Seven Sleepers and *Decius,* mentioned above, appears in the Koran (18:8) as "the men of the Cave and ar-*Raqīm.* As soon as the suggestion of Aramaic script is made, the almost perfect identity of רקים and דקיס is apparent. The problematic name in the Koran is the result of a misreading. The mistake might possibly occur in more than one variety of Aramaic script, but would have easy explanation only in the "square character" employed in the Jewish writings. Horovitz, p. 95, was inclined to doubt this solution of the long-standing riddle of "ar-Raqīm," for two reasons: (1) no other similar example of misreading has been found in the Koran; and (2) the prefixed Arabic article is unexplained. The first of these objections can hardly be termed weighty, under the circumstances; and as for the second, since *raqīm* has the form of an Arabic *adjective,* the prefixing of the article was very natural. Mohammed himself would have been especially likely to add this original touch. The coincidence is too exact to be accidental, since the hypothesis offers no difficulty at any point.

It can hardly be doubted, in view of the evidence thus far presented, that Aramaic writings were numerous in Mekka and Medina, as well as in the other Jewish centers in northwestern Arabia. I have shown that the legends of the 18th Sura were clearly obtained from a Jewish recension, and it now appears (as of course would be expected) that the language was Jewish Aramaic. Was it Mohammed himself who made the misreading Raqīm? [17] The supposition is by no means necessary, but it seems easier than any other. If the belief that he could read such a document is felt to be too difficult, it may at least be maintained that the stories had been read (translated) for him, and that he had thereafter spelled out some part for himself. As has already been said, however, the task of learning to read Aramaic would have been very easy, especially while spending much time in a bilingual community.

Concerning the Jewish Aramaic spoken in this region we have of course very little information. We do happen to know a few of its peculiarities, which doubtless were many. Dialects are easily formed, and go their own devious ways. The Hijāzī Jews were in a position very favorable for developing peculiarities of speech, both home-grown and borrowed. The nearer Christian communities made their contributions; and here, where there was comparatively little occasion for controversy, such transfer was easy. Arabian Christianity—some of it—had much in common with Judaism (Wellhausen, *Reste,* p. 200), and the influence of course worked in both directions. The Jews in southern Babylonia and Yemen, especially, took their toll of new words from their Christian or pagan neighbors, and then passed them on to the Hijaz, where not infrequently the Aramaic became Arabic. There is an interesting survival from this Hijāzī di-

---

[17] [Huber, *Die Wanderlegende,* p. 319, remarks that the use of written sources by Mohammed seems plainly suggested; yet he feels himself bound by the prevailing opinion to decide against this].

alect—a specimen of billingsgate—in one of the poems of Ḥassān ibn
Thābit, Nöldeke, *Del. Carm.*, 70, 12.[18] There is an especially opprobrious:
epithet which was applied to the Qoreish of Mekka by the adherents of
Mohammed at Medina. The poet now launches it at the enemy: *yā
saḵīna!* The meaning of the term was soon lost; the scholiast and the
native lexicons, clinging to the Arabic root, proffer a ridiculous explanation; Nöldeke notes, *originis ignotae*. It is the Aramaic שְׁחִינָא‏, "scab!"
a term of abuse not infrequently heard in modern times. The Qoreish.
were a scab, a sore, on the fair face of the Hijaz. The word was as familiar in Mekka as in Yathrib.

A few other examples of Hijāzī Aramaic—words used in meanings unknown or unusual elsewhere—can be inferred with very high probability
from the Koran. Thus זְכוּתָא, "alms," whence the Arabic *zakāt* (see
the concluding lecture); מִלָּא, "religion"; כָּפַר, "unbeliever" (see Horovitz, p. 60); פֻּרְקָן, "divine help," Arabic *furqān*,[19] certainly the term
regularly used in this sense by the Jews of this region, as occasionally
in the Targums as the rendering of Hebrew *yeshaʻ, yeshûʻā, teshûʻā.*
Very probably we should also include קְרָאן and שׁוּרָא, meaning respectively "lection" and "section" (or "chapter"). The former would
be the regular Jewish Aramaic counterpart of the Syriac *qeryān;* and
the latter could very naturally arise as a literary term designating a
"closed series" of sentences (or especially of *pesûqīm*). Both terms certainly were taken over into Arabic before Mohammed's time. It must be
remembered that he had no intention of adorning the "pure Arabic" of
his Koran with speech borrowed from any other language. He likes to
mystify by inventing strange words now and then, but that is quite another matter.[20] In such passages as 10:39; 11:16; 2:21 it is plainly implied

---

[18] [See the *Dīwān of Ḥassān ibn Thābit*, ed. Hirschfeld, CLXXV, 9; and the scholion,
p. 102].

[19] [The native interpreters of the Koran of course did not know the origin of the word,
but from the meaning of the common Arabic verb combined with such passages as 25:1 and
3.2 decided that it signified "revelation." It *never* has this meaning in the Koran, however,
but in all the cases of its occurrence signifies precisely *"divine aid."* The claim has often
been made in modern times that the word is of Christian origin, but this is absolutely out of
the question; only the *Jewish* use can explain it].

[20] [His fondness for high-sounding and perhaps unusual words is very characteristic; but

that the term *sura* is perfectly familiar to his hearers; and as for *qur'ān*, the use of the verb (imperative) in the all-important passage 96:1 shows that he thought of the verbal noun as belonging to his own language. But such technical terms in Arabic are usually of foreign origin.

An obvious peculiarity of this dialect is that—as in Syriac—the Biblical proper names which in Hebrew are written *Yisrā'ēl, Yishmā'ēl,* etc., were pronounced Isrā'ēl, Ishmā'ēl, etc. This might, of itself, have originated as a mere dialectic variation in Aramaic, without outside influence; but there is another fact to be taken into account. The Biblical proper names generally, as they occur in the Koran, are not modeled closely upon the classical Hebrew or Aramaic forms, but—as in other parts of the world—are conformed to the language of the land. The most of the names were early taken over into Arabic in forms borrowed or adapted from the neighboring regions where the inhabitants were Jewish or Christian. The Arabs of Yemen, Mesopotamia, and the Syrian border made their several contributions; and as these gained currency in the native speech, they naturally were adopted by the Jews of the Hijaz. At all events, the names were all, without exception, received by Mohammed from the Jews of Mekka, among whom they doubtless had been in use for a long time.

We happen to have evidence of the occurrence in pre-Mohammedan times of the names Ādam, Ayyūb, Dā'ūd, Sulaimān; as well as 'Ādiyā, Samau'al, Sāra, and Yuḥannā, which do not occur in the Koran (see Horovitz, *Untersuchungen,* 81 ff.). Others which probably are pre-Islamic, though the evidence is doubtful, are Ibrāhīm, Ismā'īl, Nūḥ, and Ya'qūb. And certainly these concerning which we happen to possess evidence are merely a few out of many which were in use. Hārūn (for Aharōn) antedates the Koran, as we know with certainty from the verses of 'Abbās ibn Mirdās preserved in Ibn Hishām, 661; and this doubtless is true also of its counterpart Qārūn (for Korah), concerning whom Mohammed narrates, in Sura 28:76, and probably also in 33:69, what he had learned from the haggada; as shown by Geiger, 165 f. *Fā'ūl* is a favorite form in Arabic for reproducing strange names; thus Dā'ūd, Qābūs, Fāghūr,

that he was able to recognize any of them as *of foreign origin* (Wellhausen, *Reste,* 205, note) may well be doubted].

Lā'ūdh, qāmūs (for 'Ωκεανός), and many others. The pairing of names
and other words, moreover, by fashioning a paronomastic counterpart to
an already existing form, is also thoroughly characteristic of the native
speech; it must be remembered that Mohammed did not create the Arabic
language. The pair Qābīl and Hābīl (Cain and Abel), not occurring in
the Koran and perhaps long antedating it, may serve as an example. It is
probable that Yājūj was fitted to Mājūj long before the rise of Islam; and
as for Tālūt, the "tall" king (verb *tāla*) who opposed Jālūt, this is typical
Arabian humor—of which Mohammed possessed very little. The prophet
took faithfully what he found; and he was not so simple as to make himself ridiculous in the eyes of the "people of the Book" by appearing ignorant of the well known Biblical names. I have already conjectured
(above) that the names Hārūt and Mārūt were brought to Mekka from
the Arabs at the southern border of Babylonia. The name Ilyās may have
been, as Horovitz, 82, observes, conformed to a genuine Arab name; but
it is perhaps quite as likely that it was derived from Abyssinia along with
the names Yūnus and Fir'aun, and a large number of other words which
were borrowed thence by the Arabs many generations before Islam (see
below). It often has been said that Mohammed himself "must have heard
from Christians" this or that name. Now there is no clear evidence that
Mohammed ever received anything directly from a Christian source; but
however that may be, there is no good reason for supposing that any one
of the proper names in the Koran was first introduced by him into
Hijāzī Arabic.

In the case of two of the Koranic Biblical names there may be a reasonable suspicion of error in the written transmission, either by Mohammed
or by some one of his predecessors. El-Yesa' for Elīsha' may be a mere
whimsicality of the popular oral tradition, but it is easiest to think of it
as originating in the sight, rather than the hearing, of the name. Yahyā,
for John (the Baptist), is more puzzling. Whether it is a genuine Arabian
name (as some have held) or not, it is strangely remote, in both form and
sound, from either Yohanan or 'Ιωάννης. I have long believed it probable
(with Barth, Casanova, and possibly others; see Horovitz, 167, bottom)

that the explanation is to be found in a misreading of Yuḥannā written in Arabic characters, this name being known to us as pre-Islamic.

Especially characteristic of the Jewish-Arabic dialect is the formation of curious mongrel words, partly Aramaic (or Hebrew) and partly Arabic; sometimes a legitimate mixture, at other times reminding of the whimsical creations which appear now and then in bilingual communities—as when some of the early German settlers in Pennsylvania used the word Schnecke for "snake." *Zubūr*, already mentioned, is formed on an Arabic root which bears no relation to the original Hebrew word. *Taurāt*, mentioned in the same connection, was originally written with the consonant *ya*, as though from תּוֹרְיְתָא , a mixture of Hebrew and Aramaic. *Ummī* for גוי (see above) is quite characteristic. *Māʿūn*, Sura 107:7, is the מָעוֹן of Ps. 90:1 and 71:3 interpreted by Arabic *ʿaun*. It probably was in familiar use among the Arabian Jews long before Mohammed's time. *Mathānī*, 15:87 and 39:24, is the plural of מַתְנִיתָא with the meaning "teaching." In the former passage, the numeral "seven" seems utterly inappropriate and improbable, no matter what theory of its meaning is held. I think that we have here the Aramaic סַבְעָא , and that *sabʿun min al-mathānī* was a standing phrase in the Jewish circles known to Mohammed. "We have brought you *an abundance of teachings* and the magnificent Koran" has the right sound. The peculiar employment of *sauṭ* ("whip") for "(divinely wrought) catastrophe," with the verb of "pouring out," in 89:12, also has behind it a popular Jewish-Arabic phrase, derived from the *"overflowing scourge"* (שׁוֹט) of Is. 28:15. The word *ḥanīf* has given rise to an amount of conjecture. From the way in which Mohammed employs it we may safely conclude that he heard it frequently from the Jews, and used it as they did. His idea of its meaning is best seen in 22:32, cf. also 2:129 and 3:89; it describes those who separate themselves from the worship of false gods. Abraham fled from Ur of the Chaldees as a חָנֵף , a *heretic;* and the Hijāzī Jews, connecting the word with Arabic *ḥanafa*, "to turn aside," used the Arabic adjective as a term of high praise descriptive of their great ancestor. *Hāwiya*, 101:6, one of the numerous Koranic names of "hell," is a Jewish-Arabic adaptation of the הֹוָה , "final calamity," of Is. 47:11, cf. vs.

14. See the *Oriental Studies presented to Edward G. Browne,* pp. 470 f. It is not at all likely that Mohammed himself originated the term. *Al-mu'tafikāt,* the collective name of Sodom, Gomorrah, and the cities "destroyed" with them, is a typical mixture: an Arabic form based on the *Aramaic* root אפך, reminiscent of the Hebrew usage with derivatives of הפך . Equally typical is the phrase *rabb al-'ālamīn,* which adapts a Jewish-Aramaic formula (found, in more than one form, as far back as the book of Tobit, 13:6, 10), by introducing the purely Arabic *rabb,* "Lord." Only a bilingual community could have produced this combination.

These are specimens, others might be added to the list. Besides, the Koran contains many Aramaic loanwords, most of them doubtless long current in Arabic, and not all of them of Israelite origin. It has been a favorite theory, that Mohammed mistook the meaning of not a few of the foreign words which he happened to have heard, and used them in an illegitimate way. An occasional slip of this nature would not be surprising; the use of the word *'illīyūn* (עָלְיוֹן) in 83:18 ff. seems to be an example; but in general it certainly is the case that he merely illustrates usage current in Mekka and Medina. That it is prevailingly Jewish usage is everywhere obvious. When, for example, he tells the incident of the manna and quails, using *mann* and *salwā,* we know with certainty that his narrator was one who had been brought up in the language of the Targums. It would be interesting to know in what way his curious word *yaqṭīn,* for Jonah's gourd (37:146) is related to the Hebrew קִיקָיוֹן. and whether the new creation is in any way his own. But conjecture in such a case is fruitless.

The use of the Aramaic language by the Hijāzī Israelites in their own settlements might have been taken for granted without any illustration. This was the medium of common intercourse among the Jews of the Dispersion generally; used in its various forms from Egypt and North Africa to Persia, and from Asia Minor to Italy; as universal a racial speech as Yiddish has been in modern times, and withal a literary language of high rank, though largely supplanted in this capacity by Greek in the most strongly Hellenistic regions. The Targums and the haggada went everywhere, and popular dialects, like the one now under consideration, were a matter of course. The way in which the language flourished in Italy, in the Middle Ages, is a particularly instructive example.

The Ethiopic loanwords in the Koran have often been thought to indicate one source from which Mohammed received personal instruction. A few of them, of not infrequent occurrence, belong to the religious terminology; thus *faṭara*, "create," *munāfiq*, "hypocrite," *al-hawārīyūn*, "the Apostles," and several others. Nöldeke has collected all these Koranic words, 21 in number, in his *Neue Beiträge zur semitischen Sprachwissenschaft*, 47–58; and it is easy to see from his list that only a part of them have to do with religious conceptions. To suppose that Mohammed himself had learned all these from Abyssinians would necessitate the additional supposition that he had lived for some time in an Abyssinian community, where he had learned to speak the Ethiopic language. But there are other facts to consider. There are many Ethiopic loanwords in Arabic aside from those in the Koran (see Nöldeke, *ibid.*), and something is known in regard to their origin. Siegmund Fraenkel, *Die aramäischen Fremdwörter im Arabischen*, pp. 210–216, in discussing the numerous Arabic words of Ethiopic origin dealing with ships and shipping, showed that these were a partial fruit of the long period during which the Arabs and Abyssinians were associated (as already mentioned) in charge of the traffic through the Red Sea.[20a] It was through this long and close association that at least the principal gain of Ethiopic words, the many secular and the few religious terms, was made by the Arabs, before the rise of Islam.

Mohammed had heard more than one language spoken, and seen more than one written, in his own city. The atmosphere in which he grew up was not merely commercial, nor was it by any means uncivilized. It was

---

[20a] [There is a curious reference to sea-faring Arabs in the *Futūḥ Miṣr* of Ibn 'Abd al-Ḥakam, p. 122, line 3, in the chapter dealing with the settlements of the Arab tribes in Al-Fusṭāṭ. A certain locality in the old city is said to have been occupied by the *rubbānīyūn min Ghāfiq*. Now these "sea-captains of Ghāfiq" are something of a puzzle, since this was a Syrian tribe, always far from the sea. I suspect that we have here a confusion with the Yemenite maritime town Ghalāfiqa, the well-known harbor of the city Zebīd on the Red Sea, doubtless very active in the long-continued sea traffic in company with the Abyssinians. See nevertheless, in the same work, p. 3, line 16].

at home, not in the course of any travels, that he learned what he eventually put to use. His "Arabic Koran," a work of genius, the great creation of a great man, is indeed built throughout from Arabian materials. All the properties of the Koranic diction, including the foreign words and proper names, had been familiar in Mekka before he appeared on the scene. The fundamental doctrines, as well as the terminology, were provided, and close at hand, for one who had the wisdom to see and the originality to adopt them. By good fortune, it was Israelite schooling of which he availed himself, during the years of his preparation. The teacher (or teachers) whom he frequented "morning and evening" could, unquestionably, give him by far the greater part of what we find in his new system of faith and practice for the Arabian people. The leading ideas of early Islam are all prominent in the ancient religion which he had observed, and whose teachings he had heard. Some of them, no doubt, had been familiar, as Jewish or Christian doctrine, to all the best informed Arabs of Mekka; to some extent, indeed, they had their counterpart in the native paganism. But the paramount influence of Judaism is manifest in every part of the Koran.

The One God. The strict monotheism which has always been characteristic of Islam was nowhere more sharply pronounced than in the Koran. It was not a new idea in pagan Arabia, but the extraordinary emphasis given to the doctrine by Mohammed was the result of Jewish teaching. The term *Allāh, "the* God," was already well known to the native tribesmen. There is, for instance, the familiar passage in the *mu'allaqa* of the poet Zuhair (lines 27 f.):

> Keep not from Allah what your heart enfolds,
>> Thinking 'tis hid; he knows each word and deed.
> Payment may lag, all booked and kept in store
>> For the Last Day, or vengeance come with speed.

Or the line from one of an-Nābigha's poems (*Diwan,* ed. Ahlwardt, 19, line 17b.):

> For Allah gives no man his recompense.

Ahlwardt, *Bemerkungen über die Echtheit, u.s.w.*, pronounced this poem spurious, but on quite insufficient grounds. Nöldeke has called attention, on the contrary, to the fact that the poem is addressed to a Christian prince, and that the poet is known to have had frequent intercourse with Christians.[21] This might suggest Christian origin for the use of the term "Allah" in pre-Islamic time; but the presence of a similar and long-standing monotheistic usage in pagan Arabia makes the supposition unnecessary. The ultimate origin may be neither Christian nor Hebrew.

The South Arabian inscriptions have brought to light a highly interesting parallel. In a number of them there is mention of *the* God, who is styled "the Raḥmān" (Merciful). A monument in the British Museum, deciphered by Mordtmann and D. H. Müller, is especially remarkable.[22] Here we find clearly indicated the doctrines of the divine forgiveness of sins, the acceptance of sacrifice, the contrast between this world and the next, and the evil of "associating" other deities with the Rahmān. As Margoliouth, *Relations between Arabs and Israelites,* 68, remarks, "the Qur'anic technicality *shirk,* association of other beings with Allah, whose source had previously eluded us, is here traced to its home." Moreover, we may now see a reason why Mohammed made his persistent attempt, in the Suras of the later Mekkan period, to introduce the specifically Arabian term (as he very naturally regarded it) "ar-Raḥmān" in place of "Allah," but ultimately abandoned it (17:110). It is of course to be borne in mind that the religious conceptions found in these South Arabian monuments are all ancient and widespread in western Asia, with their counterparts in the cuneiform documents as well as in the Aramaic inscriptions.

The supposition of any Christian element in Mohammed's idea of God is certainly remote. If he had ever consulted with Christians (which I find it very difficult to believe), he would presumably have heard the monophysite doctrine, which would have been likely to give him the strong impression of (at least) *two* Gods. The adoration of the Virgin Mary,

---

[21] [See my *Commercial-Theological Terms in the Koran,* p. 18, note].

[22] ["Eine monotheistische sabäische Inschrift," in the *Wiener Zeitschrift für die Kunde des Morgenlandes,* vol. X (1896), pp. 285–292].

moreover, had reached a pitch which easily accounts for the Koranic teaching (doubtless obtained from the Jews) that the Christian Trinity consisted of Allah, Mary, and Jesus (5:116; cf. 4:169, and especially 72:3). In one of the early Suras, 112, a vigorous little composition, the evil of associating others with Allah is attacked: "Say, Allah is *One;* Allah the eternal; he did not beget, nor was he begotten; nor has he any equal!" Some have interpreted this as alluding to the pagan minor deities, "daughters of Allah," mentioned in 53:19 f. But the denial of "equality" in the last verse, compared with 72:3, just mentioned, shows plainly enough that the polemic here is not against pagan worship. And the intensity of the prophet's feeling finds its most probable explanation in the Israelite reaction against the Christian doctrine.

The Written Revelation. It was from the Jews of Mekka that Mohammed learned of a divinely revealed *book.* This probably was the first great awakening and transforming idea that he received: Allah gives "guidance and help" (*hudā we-furqān*) through revelations written down by inspired men. It took hold of him with tremendous force, and started him on the path which he thenceforth followed. He himself saw portions of these heaven-sent scriptures, handled with such veneration; and he also was profoundly impressed by the intimate acquaintance with them shown by these learned men: "they know the Book as they know their own children!" (2:141, 6:20). When at length he formed the idea of the Arabian Book, he was resolved that his followers should learn it, reading half the night, if need be (73:1-4).[23] He knew—certainly he often had been told—that what he had seen and heard of the Bible was but a small part of the whole. The archetype of all holy scripture is preserved in heaven. Hence the "preserved tablet" of the Koran (85:22). St. Clair Tisdall, *The Original Sources of the Qur'an,* 119, compares Pirke Aboth v, 6, the heavenly tables of the Law. Mohammed of course had no intention of merely reproducing in the Koran, as his own revelation, any portion of what had been translated or paraphrased for his benefit. He makes one formal cita-

---

[23] [Verse 20, added later to relieve the severity of the prescription, makes it plain that the opening verses were not intended to apply to the prophet alone, but to any pious Muslim who was comfortably "wrapped up" for his night's sleep].

tion of Old Testament scripture (a very noteworthy fact), in Sura 21:105, naming its source as "az-Zabūr" (the Psalter). It is in fact from Ps. 37:29, "the righteous shall inherit the earth." With his profound conviction of his own divine appointment, he could not doubt that his advent had been predicted in the scriptures which had preceded him. He says this in more than one place, of course venturing no more than the vague assertion in regard to the Hebrew writings. The Christian scriptures were far more remote; and here he goes farther, declaring in 61:6 that Jesus foretold a coming prophet named "Ahmad." [24] This assertion may have taken shape out of Mohammed's own strong conviction, but it is perhaps more likely that he is repeating what some one had told him.[25]

It is very unlikely that Mohammed had ever seen Christian scriptures, of any sort. Certainly he never had become acquainted with their contents, beyond the few quotations and bits of legendary narrative that had reached his ear. Otherwise, with his thirst for information in religious matters, and his wish to show himself acquainted with the previous written revelations, he would have made acquisitions both significant and unmistakable, and would not have remained so profoundly ignorant of Christian history, custom, and doctrine.[26] There are three passages in the Koran which seem clearly to be dependent on the New Testament. (I have been unable to find more than these, even after carefully examining the lists provided by Rudolph and Ahrens.) The *first* is the saying in 7:38, "They (the hostile unbelievers) shall not enter paradise until the camel passes through the eye of the needle" (cf. Matt. 19:24). This a proverb which was known to both Jews and Christians everywhere. The *second* is 57:13, which immediately reminds any one who is familiar with the Gospels of the parable of the Ten Virgins, Matt. 25:1–13. This is one of the most striking, and most universal in its application, of all the popu-

[24] [Of course not "*Muhammad*," for every such prediction must have its element of mystery].

[25] [I can see no plausibility in the conjecture, first made by the Muslims (e. g. Ibn Hishām, 149 f.), and very often repeated, sometimes adorned with a play on Greek words, that the allusion is to the Gospel of John, 14:26; 16:7].

[26] [Richard Bell, *The Origin of Islam in its Christian Environment*, has an excellent chapter on Mohammed's attitude to Christianity. This subject will be considered further in the next lecture].

lar *mashalim* in the Gospels. By Mohammed's time, many who were not Christians had some knowledge of what was in the Christian scriptures. The *third* is the opening section of Sura 19, verses 1–15, which recount briefly and in poetic diction the story of the birth of John the Baptist as told in Luke 1:5–25, 57–66; a fine bit of purely Jewish narrative in the style of the Old Testament. The aged priest Zachariah, serving in the temple at Jerusalem, prays for a son and heir, though his wife is barren. He is promised a son named John, a name "not previously given." For a sign assuring the fulfilment of the promise, he is dumb for three days. As he comes forth from the temple, he makes signs to the people.

Mohammed had not himself read this account. His mistake in regard to the name "John" (cf. Luke 1:61) came from misunderstanding the man who told him the story. It is very noticeable that the correspondence with the Gospel narrative *ceases with the first chapter of Luke*. Mohammed's informant seems to have been one who was interested in the story of the priest Zachariah and the birth of John the Baptist,[27] *but not at all in the birth of Jesus*. Instead of gleaning any incidents from the second chapter of Luke, Mohammed is now, in his story of Mary and Jesus (verses 16–34), thrown entirely on his own imagination, of which he makes characteristic use. The sad blunder in vs. 29, identifying Mary with the sister of Aaron, continued in 3:30 ff. and 66:12, is the result of his own ignorant combination, not what any other had told him. It is a fair conjecture that each and all of these three bits of Gospel tradition were delivered to him by his Jewish teachers. There is no difficulty in the supposition, and no other seems quite plausible.

The Prophet, and the Chosen People. Mohammed's doctrine of the *nabī* and his mission was fundamental, one of the few supremely important ideas in Islam. And this, again, the conception of *the prophet* as the final authority on earth, he could only have obtained from Israelite sources. The whole history of Israel centered in prophets. In each successive stage, one of these divinely appointed men was the vice-gerent of God. They were the true leaders of all worldly affairs, for they alone possessed the direct revelation; kings held a relatively lower place. Ques-

[27] [Mohammed tells the story again in 3:33 ff., besides alluding to it in 21:89 f.].

tions of high importance and great difficulty could only be settled "when a prophet should arise." After Mohammed came to the persuasion that the Arabs must have their prophet, the idea of the authority of this vice-gerent grew steadily. In the older parts of the Koran it is Allah who must be obeyed; in the Medina chapters it is almost everywhere "Allah *and his prophet*."

What God intended from the beginning to give out to mankind he gave piecemeal, each time through some one prophet to the men of his genera-tion. According to the Israelite tradition, each of the many portions of Hebrew scripture was written by a prophet, a "man of the Book"—as Mohammed declares, for example, of John (Yaḥyā), in 19:13. Moreover, these human depositories of the divine wisdom were all members of a single great family. In all Mohammed's contact with his Israelite teachers he had been impressed with the idea of *the chosen people*. This, again, laid hold of him mightily, and brought forth his conception of the great mission of the Arabs. Allah had selected, once for all, the family of Abra-ham. Israel (which for Mohammed of course included the Christians) had had its day, and it was now the turn of Ishmael. On this other branch of the family rested the final choice, and he, Mohammed, was the final prophet.

All of the Koran was sent from heaven, he believed. As for the fits, or seizures, resembling epilepsy, out of which he brought forth some of the "messages" received in times of most urgent need, I have long believed that they were obtained through self-hypnotism. Before Mohammed made his public claim to prophecy, he had acquired the technique of this ab-normal mental condition; in the same way in which countless others have gained it, namely through protracted fasting, vigils, and excited meditation. The first fit, or fits, came upon him unawares, and he recog-nized a heaven-sent answer to his searchings of heart. As usual in such cases, the means of producing the states came more and more completely under his control; and he used them, in good faith, as a divine gift. After the paroxysm, through which he believed himself to receive illumination from above, followed a struggle with the ideas and phrases of the desired "message," until at last it was worked into shape. Whatever form of words

Mohammed thus decided upon was the one to which he was guided by the angel of revelation; of this he was fully persuaded, and his right to give it forth he never doubted. The well known phenomena of self-hypnotism agree strikingly with the description of Mohammed's "fits" given by his biographers. See especially Otto Stoll, *Suggestion und Hypnotismus*, 2te Aufl., Leipzig, 1904, pp. 256–258; also John Clark Archer, *Mystical Elements in Mohammed* (diss.), New Haven, Yale Press, 1924, pp. 71–74, 87; and my essay, "Mysticism in Islam," in Sneath's *At One with the Invisible*, Macmillan, 1921, pp. 144–146.

Other Doctrines. The leading themes of the prophet's early preaching, those on which he chiefly relied to make an impression on his hearers, whether city dwellers or nomad tribesmen, were each and all characteristic features of Judaism. The resurrection of all men, both the just and the unjust; an idea familiar at least since Dan. 12:2 f., and always powerfully influential. The Judgment Day, *yōm dīnā rabbā,* when the "books" are opened, and every man is brought to his reckoning. The reward of heaven, the "garden," and the punishment of hell, with the everlasting fire of *Gēhinnām;* ideas which Mohammed of course enriched mightily from his own imagination. The doctrine of angels and evil spirits; in particular the activities of Iblīs, and of Gabriel, the angel of revelation. Mohammed must have been profoundly impressed by the first chapter of Genesis, judging from the amount of space given in the Koran to the creation of heaven and earth, of man, and of all the objects of nature. He may or may not have heard the verse Micah 6:8; at all events, he reiterates in his earliest Suras the primal duties of man: belief in Allah, humanity, and fair dealing.

The doctrines listed above are all equally characteristic of Christianity; but it was not from Christians that the Arabian prophet obtained them. These beliefs, and the many others connected with them, could not be acquired, and digested, in a few days, or in a few months; and it is utterly impossible to suppose that Mohammed ever had any *continuous* intercourse with Christians. He has some scattered information—a considerable amount, though generally vague or fantastic—*about* Christian beliefs, and has been told numerous things which occur in Christian scriptures; but of the basal, omnipresent conceptions, the matters of chief popular interest, the polemical theses (against the Jews, for example), characteristic of that religion, even in its crudest forms, he has not an inkling. With Judaism, on the contrary, his acquaintance is intimate and many-sided. He learned his lessons well; and when a thoroughgoing comparison is made of the Koranic material, of all sorts, with the standard Hebrew-Jewish writings then current, we must say with emphasis that his authorities, whoever they were, were men well versed in the Bible, the oral law, and the haggada.

ALLAH AND ISLAM IN ANCIENT HISTORY

The lessons which Mohammed learned, in one way or another, from the Israelites of Mekka gave him a new horizon. The idea of the prophet and his mission and authority, and the picture of the chosen people holding the religious leadership of the nations of the earth, illustrated in the written records of the past from the very beginning, meant more to the Mekkan tradesman than any other of his acquisitions. He not only gained a new conception of human history, but began to see that it is all religious history, directed in its successive periods by Allah and his prophets. The choice of the Arabs was one link in a continuous chain, and the revelation given to them through their prophet was the last stage in a process which began with Adam. Moreover, the thought of "Islām" (whenever this took shape in Mohammed's mind) must take in not only the Arabs, but also the other peoples of the earth. Allah had not simply transferred his interest from the children of Israel (i. e. the Jews and Christians) to the children of Ishmael; he was the "Lord of the Worlds," holding all races in his hand. The preferred people has a certain responsibility for its fellows. The Hebrew scriptures took account of foreign nations, and assigned them to their places with authority; the prophets were much concerned with them; Jonah was sent to Nineveh to convert its population. The great table in the tenth chapter of Genesis (of which Mohammed certainly had some knowledge) classified the races of the earth according to their genealogy.

All this was food for the Arabian prophet's thought, but not material for his use. He had neither the knowledge of the outside world nor the interest in it which would lead him to make his Koran range abroad. The idea of a sketch of religious history, connected or disconnected, could hardly have occurred to him, nor would any such undertaking have served his purpose. His concern was with the Arabs, with the Israelites whose inheritance they had received, and especially with the Hebrew prophets as his own predecessors. The one and only place in which the Koran ventures outside Arabia, either in connection with events of its own day or in prophecy of the future, is the remarkable passage at the beginning of the 30th Sura, where the prophet takes momentary notice of a contemporary event in Syria, a military incident in the Graeco-Persian war about which some information had reached Mekka: "The Greeks are beaten, in a near part of the land; but after their defeat they themselves shall conquer, in a few years." This singular prediction is probably not a *vaticinium ex eventu* (though the Greeks *did* ultimately conquer), but the expression of the prophet's conviction that the "people of the Book" were bound to triumph over the unbelievers.

The "history" contained in the Koran consists mainly of bits of narration taken from the Old Testament and the Jewish midrash. This fragmentary material, usually scattered along in the most casual way, occupies a large portion of the growing volume, especially the part produced in the middle years of the prophet's public career. The earliest Suras, prevailingly brief, consist chiefly of impassioned exhortation. Mohammed is here the preacher, proclaiming, warning, and promising. In the last years of his life, at Medina, he is so occupied with legislation and other practical matters as to leave little room for story telling, even if that which he regarded as essential had not already been provided. It is during the latter years of his Mekkan ministry, especially, that he gives a large amount of space to the "old stories" (as his skeptical countrymen impolitely termed them). He himself was highly interested in the tales of the ancients, the wonders which Allah wrought among them, the deeds and experiences of their famous men, from Adam and his family down to the Seven Sleepers of Ephesus and the martyrs of Nejrān. The Arabs must now be told all this, and learn it as the preliminary stage of their own religious history.

Moreover, the stories would help him to gain a hearing. Thus he says at the beginning of the twelfth Sura, dealing with Joseph and his fortunes, "We now narrate to you a most beautiful tale." [28] And in fact, these little anecdotes of prophets and heroes undoubtedly led many to listen who otherwise would have paid no attention to the new teacher.

Mohammed was both sincere and wise in his effort to give the new religion of the Arabs its secure foundation in the past, and to claim its affiliation with the great religions which had preceded. And he had in mind, in his constant reference to Biblical personages and incidents, not merely the instruction and inspiration of his countrymen, but also the effect on another audience. The ideas which had awakened him and changed his whole view of life were not his own discovery, but were the fruits of his intercourse with the Jews of Mekka, possibly (though not probably) also with Christians, either at home or abroad. These counsellors should hear the revelation now given by Allah to his Arabian prophet. In Mohammed's thought, Islam was not at all a new religion, but merely a continuation. The Koran, he declares many times over, "confirms" the scriptures already existing. Jews and Christians (he hardly distinguished between them at first) would be glad to hear more about Moses and Solomon and Jesus. He felt that he was giving them support, and expected them to support him in return.

There was another consideration which weighed heavily. The history of the past, from beginning to end, was the story of his own predecessors. He was filled with the thought of those favored men who stood so near to the One God, and by him had been commissioned to teach their people. They were "prophets" (*nebīyīm, anbiyā'*) one and all, and the fact ever foremost in his mind was the way in which their message had been received, or rather rejected, by the most of their contemporaries. His own experience, as soon as he had fairly begun preaching to the people of Mekka, showed him very clearly what opposition a prophet is likely to encounter. The new teaching is not received with gratitude and awe; it is laughed at. Thus Noah was ridiculed by his people, until they were drowned in the flood. So the men of Sodom and Gomorrah jeered at Lot,

[28] [Formally these words are said by the angel Gabriel to Mohammed].

until the fire came down from heaven. The Israelites of the exodus from Egypt would not submit to the authority of Moses, but rebelled against him; and for their obduracy they perished in the desert. In general, the Hebrew prophets were very badly treated; so Mohammed's informants told him. It is easy to see why the Koran abounds in passages dealing with the heroes and patriarchs of the Old Testament. There are lessons here "for those who have intelligence," the Mekkan prophet keeps reiterating. The truth prevailed, in spite of opposition; the unbelievers roasted in Gehennama; and—most important of all—the religion proclaimed by these ancient mouthpieces of God is precisely the one which is now announced, in its final and most perfect form, to the people of Arabia.

There were also lessons from Arabian history. Mohammed and his fellow-countrymen had seen the ruins of vanished cities, and had heard of many others. There were traditions of the *sail al-'arim* (34, 15), the bursting of the great dam at Ma'rib in Yemen, and the destruction of the city by the resulting flood. This was a judgment from heaven. Far more striking were the signs of vanished splendor, of a high civilization now utterly obliterated, in the regions north of the Hijaz. The tribes of 'Ād and Thamūd, and the cities of Midian had perished, leaving behind only a few very impressive traces. Why were these prosperous peoples wiped out of existence? Mohammed's imagination gave the answer. Each one of them had its prophet, who preached Islām. They would not hear, and therefore God destroyed them. But the Koranic narratives dealing with these events were, after all, of secondary importance. Islām was for the world, and the emphasis must be laid on persons and events which were known and acknowledged the world over. The three rejected prophets of the northern desert and Sinai were indeed important in Mohammed's scheme of religious history, but they were small links in a great chain. When the merchants of Qoreish traveled into Egypt, Syria, Mesopotamia, and Abyssinia, they would meet no one who had ever heard of Hūd, or Ṣāliḥ, or Shu'aib; but in every city where they halted they would find multitudes to whom the names of Noah, Abraham, Joseph, David, Elijah, and "Jesus the son of Mary" were perfectly familiar.

A very striking feature of the Koranic scraps of Israelite history is the rabbinic element—gleanings from Talmud and midrash—so frequently in evidence. This has always been the subject of comment and conjecture. Thus H. P. Smith, *The Bible and Islam*, p. 77, says of Mohammed's story of Moses, "From Jewish tradition he asserts: that Moses refused all Egyptian nurses; that the people at Mount Sinai demanded to see God, and on seeing him fell dead, but were revived by divine power; and that they refused to accept the covenant until the mountain was lifted up bodily and held over them (28: 11; 2: 53, 60; 7: 170). The information that the golden calf, through the magic of its maker, *bellowed*, is found in rabbinical sources." Geiger, *Was hat Mohammed . . . . aufgenommen?*, pp. 154–172, had discussed these and other similar features of the story. The remark is made in Nöldeke-Schwally, p. 8, that the source of Mohammed's knowledge of Biblical characters and events was less the Bible than the extra-canonical literature. This, I think, states the matter not quite correctly, for even in the stories where Mohammed makes largest use of the haggada there is frequent evidence that he knew also the canonical account. Wellhausen, *Reste* (1st ed.), p. 205, in his argument for the Christian origin of Islam, handles this Jewish haggada in a very gingerly manner. "Es ist wahrscheinlich, dass Muhammed denselben durch jüdische Vermittlung zugeführt bekommen hat, wenngleich man dessen eingedenk bleiben muss, dass derselbe Segensstoff auch bei den orientalischen Christen im Umlauf war, und dass die Haggada ihre Quelle grossenteils in apokryphen Schriften hatte, die wenn sie auch jüdischen Ursprungs waren doch seit dem zweiten Jahrhundert immer ausschliesslicher in christlichen Besitz übergingen." I confess myself unable to see light in this argument, nor do I know any sound reason for doubting that Mohammed received his haggada directly from Jews. Wellhausen felt this to be a weak point; for he at once proceeds to draw a line between the *religious* material of the Koran and the *stories*, which he would have us believe to be merely the fruit of the prophet's intellectual curiosity. It therefore, he declares, is a matter of very little importance, whence Mohammed obtained the legends; and the fact that some "chance" brought him into contact with a man who was acquainted with Jewish lore is not really significant. To this, an advocate of the contrary view would reply, that the legends are the "Vorgeschichte" of Islam; the account of Allah's dealing with men in the past, from which may be learned something in regard to his dealing in the present; the indispensable fabric of the doctrine of "the prophet of Allah." And if it was by mere "chance" that Mohammed was given Israelite instruction, it was a chance that lasted many years, and gave the Koran the most, and the best, of its material.

Mohammed's heroes of the past are almost all designated by him as "prophets"; they received the truth from Allah, and taught it to their children and their contemporaries. Adam was a prophet (20:120; 3:30); so were Ishmael, and David, and Job. In all, twenty-five are named; among them are the three Arabian prophets, Hūd, Ṣāliḥ, and Shu'aib, and the three from the Gospel: Zachariah, John the Baptist, and Jesus. All the rest are from the Old Testament. A list of eighteen, containing only Biblical names, is given in Sura 6:83–86. In 33:7 there is an instructive list of the most important of the prophets, those with whom Allah made a special covenant. The names are these: Mohammed, Noah, Abraham, Moses, and Jesus. (The fact that Mohammed is named first is due merely to the literary form of the passage.) It is very noticeable that the Koran knows nothing of Isaiah, Jeremiah, and Ezekiel, nor has knowledge of any of the Minor Prophets with the exception of Jonah. This certainly does not mean that the books of these prophets were wanting at Mekka, but simply, that they were utterly beyond Mohammed's comprehension and outside his interests. His instructors knew better than to try to introduce him to these abstruse writings. Jonah, the little story-book, was in a class by itself. We might indeed have expected to find some mention of Daniel; but he also, it seems, did not enter Mohammed's horizon.

It must always be borne in mind that we cannot tell with certainty, from the Koran, what portions of the Old Testament the prophet had heard. He makes use only of what is important for his purpose, as we learn from an occasional allusion to persons or events not otherwise treated. As a matter of fact, he shows some acquaintance with each of the five books of the Torah, and with the "historical books" from Joshua to 2 Kings. The book of Joshua, indeed, is represented only in the person of the prophet Dhu 'l-Kifl, who will receive notice presently; while a bit of the book of Judges, taken from the story of Gideon, has strayed into the narrative of "Saul and Goliath" (see the Fourth Lecture). Barely mentioned, for instance, are Āzar, named in 6:74 as the father (!) of Abraham (evidently el-Āzar, derived from the Eliezer of Gen. 15:2); 'Imrān (Amram), named as the father of Moses, Aaron, and Miriam (identified with the Virgin Mary); Samuel, introduced without name as the prophet who anointed Saul as king; Elijah and Elisha. Also the wives of Noah, Lot, and Pharaoh, of whom the first two are assigned to everlasting fire. The influence of the Jewish haggada constantly appears. Rabbinical sources for the Koranic narratives of Cain, Noah, Lot, and Aaron have been pointed out by Geiger, and others are soon to be mentioned. For a few interesting bits of legend which sound like Jewish lore—the incident of the Breakers of the Sabbath, who were changed to apes (2:61; 4:50; 5:65; 7:166); David's invention of coats of mail (21:80); and how Job produced a spring of cool water by stamping on the ground, and thereafter was permitted to fulfil his hasty oath by beating his wife with a bundle of leaves instead of with a rod (38:41–43)—no haggadic source is known.

Mohammed did his best with *Arabian* religious history, though he had little at hand that he could use. He thought of Hūd, the prophet of the people 'Ād, Ṣāliḥ, the prophet of Thamūd, and perhaps especially Shu'aib, the prophet of Midian, as preachers sent to peoples very closely related to the Arabs; and he introduces them frequently, sometimes in passages of considerable length, in the Suras of the Mekkan period. The incident of the elephant brought to the neighborhood of Mekka by the army of Abraha, the Abyssinian viceroy of Yemen, at about the middle of the sixth century, is made the subject of the very early Sura 105, as an example of the might of Allah, who "brought their cunning plans to nought." In another Sura of about the same time there is mention of "the Men of the Ditch, of the blazing fire; when they sat above it, witnessing what they were doing to the believers" (85:4–7). I have no doubt, in spite of the arguments of Geiger (p. 189) and Horovitz (pp. 92 f.), that this refers to the persecution of the Christians of Nejrān by the Yemenite Jewish ruler Dhū Nuwās, shortly before the time of the viceroy Abraha.[29] It seems quite plain that the Koran is dealing here with a historical event, and persecution for religious faith is clearly stated in vs. 8. Mohammed treats the story as something well known in Mekka.

There is another feature of Arabian history, seemingly remote from Israelite influence, which occupied Mohammed's attention. There were certain ancient practices, religious and social, which were deeply imbedded in the life of the people; the property not merely of the Hijaz, but of the Arabian peninsula. The customs and ceremonies connected with the Ka'ba at Mekka had much to do with the commercial and friendly intercourse of the tribes, and the "house" itself was venerated far and wide. We may be sure that Mohammed intended, from the first, to preserve every time-honored element of the native "paganism" which did not involve idolatry. Neither the people of Mekka and Yathrib and Ṭā'if, nor the Bedouin tribesmen, would have been willing to abandon their ancestral rites and practices for no obviously compelling reason; and Mohammed would have been the last man to wish them to do so. It was imperative for his scheme of things to plant the new religion as deeply in the soil of Arabia as in that of the Hebrew and Christian revelations. This he could do by the help of the patriarch Ishmael, as will appear.

It is not necessary to review here the long list of personages of ancient history whose names and deeds play so important a part in the Koran. A considerable part of the Hebrew history and haggadic legend thus reproduced will be touched upon in the course of the next Lecture, dealing with the Koranic narratives. At that time (if Allah wills) a goodly number of Biblical characters (including Alexander the Great) will be introduced in their Arabian dress; so that sooner or later all the members of the "long list" shall have received mention, at least by name. Some of this Jewish-Muslim material has been well treated by Geiger, other writers have occupied themselves chiefly or wholly with the post-Mohammedan legends, as for example Weil's *Biblische Legenden der Muselmänner,* 1845 (also translated into English), and the important essays by Max

[29] [See Axel Moberg, *The Book of the Himyarites* (Lund, 1924)].

Grünbaum and Israel Schapiro. The proper names in the Koran have been admirably treated by Josef Horovitz in his article, "Jewish Proper Names and Derivatives in the Koran," in the *Hebrew Union College Annual*, II (1925), 145–184, and again in the Second Part of his *Koranische Untersuchungen* (1926).

The present Lecture will pay especial attention to two subjects which are of prime importance for our understanding of the foundations of Islam: the source of Mohammed's ideas regarding Jesus and the Christian religion, and the place occupied by Abraham and Ishmael in his conception of the revelation to the Arabs. Before dealing with these three "prophets," however, I shall notice very briefly a few others, for whom the mere mention by name seems, for one reason or another, hardly sufficient.

It is perhaps needless to say, that the Hebrew chronology of the Koran is not one of its strong points. Mohammed had some idea of the long time that must have elapsed since Moses; though he certainly knew nothing of the complete line of descent which the Muslim genealogists carried back from his family, and from the Arab tribes generally, to Adam and Eve. He knew, as early (at least) as the 37th Sura, something of the succession of Hebrew heroes, and was aware that the prophet-kings, Saul, David, and Solomon, were subsequent to the patriarchs; however hazy his ideas were as to the order of the other prophets and the time at which they lived. He had fantastic notions (as others have had) in regard to Ezra, and evidently had no idea where to locate him. Elijah and Elisha, Job, Jonah, and "Idrīs," are left by him floating about, with no secure resting place. He had heard nothing whatever as to the genealogy of Jesus (the claimed descent from David), nor of his contemporaries (excepting the family of John the Baptist), nor of any Christian history. He associated Moses with Jesus, evidently believing that very soon after the revelation to the Hebrew law-giver there had followed the similar revelation which had produced the Christians and their sacred book. This appears in his identification of Mary the mother of Jesus with Miriam the sister of Moses and Aaron, plainly stated in more than one place. In all this there is nothing surprising, when it is remembered how the prophet received his information.

A Few "Minor" Prophets. The incident in the life of *Adam* which is oftenest dwelt upon in the Koran is the refusal of the devil (*Iblīs, Shaiṭān*) to obey the divine command to the angels to fall down before this newly created being. The account is best given in 38:73–77, and appears only less fully in six other passages. Geiger, p. 98, doubts whether this can have come to Mohammed through Jewish tradition, on the ground that the command to worship any other than God would have seemed to any Israelite inconceivable. Grünbaum, *Neue Beiträge zur semitischen Sagenkunde,* pp. 60 f., follows Geiger. The Koran does not speak of *worshipping,* however, but merely of approaching a personage of high rank in a truly oriental way. See, for example, the use of the verb in the last verse of 'Amr ibn Kulthūm's *muʻallaqa* (Arnold's *Septem Moʻallaḳāt,* p. 144), where the action is one of purely human homage. The passages which Geiger cites, *Sanhedrin* 59 b (not "29") and *Midr. Rabba* 8, are a sufficient parallel to the Koran. See also the "Life of Adam and Eve" (Charles, *Apocrypha and Pseudepigrapha*), chaps. 12–17. As for Iblīs and ash-Shaiṭān, the former name seems to have come down into Arabia from the north, while the latter is evidently a fruit of the long contact with the Abyssinians; both names were doubtless current among the Jews of the Hijaz before Mohammed's time. The identification of the serpent with Satan would seem to be implied in the passage *Ber. Rabba* 17, which Geiger quotes. See also Ginzberg, *Legends of the Jews,* V, p. 84.

The prophet *Shuʻaib,* who was sent to the Midianites, is generally recognized as identical with the Biblical Jethro. The name was hardly invented by Mohammed; it is far more likely that it was brought into use by the Arabian Jews. Its origin is obscure, but it is natural to suppose that there was some etymological reflection behind it. These Midianites, from whom Moses took his wife (the daughter of a priest), were in their origin very closely related to the Hebrews, though *their main body* became a persistent and dangerous enemy. Might the name Shuʻaib, "little tribe," have been the result of thinking of יִתְרוֹ ("rest of it") as representing the faithful "remainder" of a larger Hebrew tribe?

The prophet *Dhū 'l-Kifl* presents another problem. I think that here again the solution is to be found in the long association of the Arabs with the Abyssinians, in the traffic on the Red Sea. The word *kefl* appears frequently in the Ethiopic version of Joshua in speaking of the "division" of the territory among the Hebrew tribes, which is the central feature of that book. I believe that Joshua is "Dhū 'l-Kifl," that is, the one who effected the Division. It is very noticeable that he does not receive mention in the Koran, unless under this name.

'Uzair ("little Ezra") is made by Mohammed the subject of a very singular accusation aimed at the Jews. In one of the latest Suras, and in a context dealing harshly with all those who are not Muslims, occurs this passage (9:30): "The Jews say, Ezra ('Uzair) is the son of God, and the Christians say, el-Mesīaḥ is the son of God." (This might make Ezra turn in his grave—if he had one.) Mohammed here seems to be trying to believe what some enemy of the Jews had told him. He is bound to claim pure monotheism for the Muslims alone, in his day. The use of the unpleasant diminutive, *"little* Ezra," is probably his own invention. The name occurs nowhere else; and this great figure in Jewish legend has no other mention in the Koran, unless under the name which here follows.

If I am not mistaken, Ezra has his double in the Koran, in the person of the prophet *Idrīs* (19:57 f., 21:85), of whom we are told only this, that he was given a high place of honor. The name has generally been derived from Ἔσδρας; and indeed, it could hardly be anything else. Various other suggestions have been made, from Nöldeke's "Andreas" (*Zeitschrift für Assyriologie,* vol. 17, 83 ff.) to Toy's "Theodore of Mopsuestia." But any Andreas seems utterly remote from Mohammed's horizon. On the other hand, it would be very easy for the Greek name of the famous Ezra to make its way down into Arabia, there ultimately to be picked up by the Arabian prophet. The latter could of course not be expected to know, or to find out, that it was only another name for his " 'Uzair."

'Īsā ibn Maryam. The treatment which Jesus and his work receive in the Koran is of especial importance in the attempt to determine the principal sources of Mohammedanism. It is a patent fact that the prophet knew next to nothing about Jesus; also, that there are no distinctly and peculiarly

Christian doctrines in the sacred book. All those who have studied the matter know and declare that the great bulk of the Koranic material is of Jewish origin; and we have certain knowledge that Mohammed resorted habitually to learned Jewish teachers. Have we any good reason for supposing that he also received personal instruction from a Christian? I believe that it will eventually be recognized that whatever knowledge (or pseudo-knowledge) he possessed in regard to the person and life òf Jesus was derived from two sources: *first,* the facts and fancies which were common property in the Hijaz and elsewhere in Arabia; and *second,* a small amount of information supplied to him by his Israelite mentors.

The form of the name is remarkable, in comparison with Yēshū'. The Christian Arabs of northern Arabia had the form Yāsū',[30] which is just what would be expected; " 'Īsā" makes its first appearance in the Koran. It has been explained by Nöldeke and others as a Jewish pleasantry of which Mohammed was the innocent victim, the name of *Esau,* the typical enemy, being in fact substituted for that of Jesus.[31] There is indeed complete formal identity, and the symbolic transfer is certainly characteristic. The Mekkan Israelite who might be supposed to have had this happy thought can of course have had no idea that the substituted name would go beyond Mohammed ibn Abdallah and his few adherents. There is another explanation, which in recent years has frequently been adopted. The pronunciation of the name in Nestorian Syriac is *Išo'* (אִישׁוֹעַ). It is surmised that when this pronunciation came (in some way) to Mohammed's ear, he altered it by transposing the guttural and changing the final vowel, in order (for some reason) to give it assonance with the name Mūsā (Moses).[32] This theory, while neither simple nor free from difficulties, is not quite impossible, and the student may take his choice.

If the hypothesis of the Syriac origin of the name is entertained, it

---

[30] [See the references in Horovitz, *Untersuchungen,* p. 129].

[31] [See the ZDMG., vol. 41, p. 720, and the *Encyclopaedia of Islam,* s.v. " 'Īsā"].

[32] [This explanation is at least as old as the year 1861 (see Rudolph, p. 67, note 25). See also the references in Horovitz, *Untersuchungen,* 128 f. Rudolph would explain the supposed pairing of Jesus with Moses on the ground that each of the two was the founder of a religion. But Mohammed did not by any means regard Moses as a "Religionsstifter"; he was a lawgiver—which Jesus was not. A more plausible ground might be seen in the simple fact that both were members of the family of 'Imrān].

certainly is permissible to give it connection with that one of Mohammed's habitual instructors (the only one concerning whom we have any
definite information) who seems to have come to Mekka from the Persian
or Babylonian domain. This man has been mentioned several times in the
preceding lectures. His language was *'ajamī*. He was certainly a learned
man, probably a Jew, certainly *not* a Christian (see below). The passage
in which he is mentioned (16:105) is late Mekkan, and it is evident that
Mohammed had for some time been under his instruction. A number of
Koranic properties which seem to have come from Mesopotamia make
their appearance at about this time. Such are the Babylonian angels
Hārūt and Mārūt, the pair Yājūj and Mājūj (both pairs already noticed),
the mention of the Ṣābians," and the collection of Mesopotamian-Jewish
legends utilized in the 18th Sura; see especially the Fourth Lecture. It is
at least very noticeable that the first mention of 'Īsā in the Koran, in the
19th Sura, dates from this same period.

Rudolph, p. 64, remarks on the strange circumstance that the earliest
occurrence of the name of Jesus in the Koran comes so late. It is indeed
significant! In general, it is not safe to conclude that the prophet's first
knowledge of a Biblical personage or conception of an idea may be dated
from the Koran, and chronological tables assigning such matters to successive periods are likely to be of slight value. But if, as Rudolph supposes,
Mohammed had received his earliest and most important religious en-
lightenment from Christians, it is nothing short of amazing that his only
allusion to anything specifically Christian, prior to the second Mekkan
period, should be an incidental rebuke of the worship of two Gods. He
had of course from the first some knowledge of the Christian sect (as he
would have termed it), and may have heard the name of its founder. In
one of his early Suras (112) he attacks the worship of "Allah's son," but
the doctrine was too remote to give him any real concern, and he exhibits
no further interest in it until the later period when he began to hear more
about this "prophet" and his history. And even in the Suras of the Medina
period it is evident that the Christians, with their founder and their
beliefs, were only on the outer edge of his horizon, not at all important for

the basal doctrines of Islam, and chiefly useful in the polemic against the Jews.

Wellhausen, in his too hasty contention that the Arabian prophet received his first and chief impulse from Christianity, made the strange claim that Mohammed assigned to Jesus the supreme place in the religious history of the past. "Jüdische Gesinnung verrät es nicht, dass Jesus im Quran hoch über alle Propheten des Alten Testamentes gestellt wird" (*Reste,* 1887, p. 205). This assertion evidently rests on a slip of the memory, or on forced interpretation, for there is in the Koran nothing that could substantiate it. On the contrary, in 2:130, a passage belonging to the Medina period, where the prophets, Jesus among them, are enumerated by name or collectively, the words are added: "We make no distinction among them." That is, in rank; certain prophets, or groups of prophets, were endowed with special gifts or distinctions not shared by their fellows (2:254). Abraham was given Islām (2:126; 22:77); Moses was given *The Book* (2:81); David was given the Psalms (4:161); Jesus was given the wondrous signs (*bayyināt*) and "the Spirit" (2:81, 254). The five prophets with whom Allah made a special covenant—Jesus among them—have already been named (Sura 33:7). Nowhere in the Koran is there any trace of a wish to give 'Īsā ibn Maryam especially high rank among the prophets; he simply had his very honorable place (chronologically somewhat vague!) in the long line. *Later,* in the early caliphate, when Muslims and Christians were closely associated, especially in Syria and Egypt, Jesus was indeed placed "high above the prophets of the Old Testament," and the attempt was made to interpret the Koran accordingly, as any one may learn by reading the native commentators.

Mohammed did his best to specify the particular distinctions which Jesus had been given, as a prophet; and he had cogent reason for so doing, quite aside from any polemic against the Jews. The fact of a great Christian world outside was perfectly familiar in all the cities of Arabia. The purpose of the newly arisen Arabian prophet was, from the first, to gain the support of the Jews and the Christians, by no means to make them his enemies. His program was obviously and necessarily this, to declare that these faiths, in their beginnings and as promulgated by their founders and divinely appointed representatives, were identical with his own teaching. Only in their later development had they strayed from the right path. The time had come for a new prophet to call these peoples back to the true religion. This could only be done by exalting their teachers and claiming to build on their foundation. Many since Mohammed's time have conceived the same plan, though lacking his energy and his unique opportunity. During the first years of his public teaching, however, as has already been said and many scholars have remarked, he seems to have known so little about the Christians that he could simply class them as Israelites who had gone their own peculiar way.

It was with Abyssinia especially that the Mekkans associated the Christian faith. Arabs and Abyssinians were, and from ancient time had been, partners in the Red Sea traffic; and, as we have seen, scraps of Abyssinian speech and religious terminology had made their way all over the peninsula. It was very well known that the Christians worshipped al-Masīḥ. This name is attested in Arabia before Mohammed's time, all the way from Nejrān in the south to Ghassān in the north (Horovitz, pp. 129 f.); and he eventually employs it frequently in the Koran. Accompanying this term was another, ar-Rūḥ, "the Spirit," associated in some way with the worship of Jesus and regularly mentioned along with him. Mohammed was utterly bewildered by the term (and so, of course, were the Arabs generally, in so far as it was known to them), and he plays with it in the Koran in several very different ways. Stories of the miracles of Jesus, including the raising of the dead, we should suppose to have been what the Arabs heard first and oftenest from their Abyssinian associates, and indeed from all other Christians with whom they came in contact. The fact that the Koran has no mention of these "bayyināt" until the second Mekkan period is merely another indication of the comparative remoteness of the Christians and their doctrines from the prophet's earlier thinking. When at length they became somewhat more real to him, he picked up the few Christian terms that were lying ready to hand, and used them over and over, with only the vaguest ideas as to their meaning. (Even Rudolph, p. 65, reaches a similar conclusion: "Bei den dürftigen Kenntnissen, die er speziell von Jesus hat, bekommt man den Eindruck, dass er sich seine Anschauung aus Einzelheiten, die er da und dort erfuhr, selbst zusammengemacht hat".)

As to the *time* when the prophet began to feel more directly concerned with the claims of the Christians, it is a plausible conjecture that it coincided with the so-called "Abyssinian migration" which took place about five years after the beginning of his public activity. Ahrens, p. 150, thinks that this shows that Mohammed felt himself in closer sympathy with Christianity than with Judaism: "hätte er sich dem Judentume näher verwandt gefühlt, so lag für ihn der Anschluss an die Juden von Jathrib oder Khaibar näher." On the contrary, the reason for Mohammed's choice is obvious; namely, that while still in Mekka he had been shown very clearly that the Jews were much more likely to be his enemies than his friends. The time had come when he and his followers needed to see what support could be had from the Christians; but it is hardly likely that the envoys—or fugitives—went with high hopes. While the Muslim accounts are utterly incredible in the most of their details, the main fact seems well established, namely, that a company of Mohammed's adherents took temporary refuge in Abyssinia; partly in protest against the treatment which they had received in Mekka, partly also, no doubt, in the hope of receiving some support—at least moral support—from these time-honored allies. It was a most natural proceeding, and it doubtless made an impression in Mekka, though not in Abyssinia. The gain which the Koran made from it seems to have been merely what has just been described, an awakening of interest which led the prophet to gather up such Christian scraps as he could use. One of the new catchwords was *"Injil"* (Evangelium), which in Mohammed's mouth—as Rudolph, p. 80, remarks—meant simply the Christian book of revelation preserved in heaven; he seems to have known nothing about separate gospels or evangelists. He took up the shibboleth of the Virgin Birth (21:91; 66:12); this also he could concede to the Christians without difficulty, and he maintains it stoutly in opposition to the Jews (4:155). Nevertheless Jesus was a mere man like other men (16:45; 21:7); the Koran says this in different ways, in numerous passages. Whether "the Word" (*kalima,* λόγος) as a designation of Jesus, 3:40 and elsewhere, was only another catchword which Mohammed could of himself pick up in Mekka or Medina may be strongly doubted. He had among his teachers in Mekka a man of letters who had read at least some portion of the Gospels and was familiar with the popular legends regarding Jesus which were current in Christian lands; and it was from him, in all probability, that he heard the theological term. This man was a learned Jew, as I think the evidence plainly shows.

It has sometimes been said, e. g. recently by Rudolph, pp. 65 f., and Ahrens, p. 153, that a Jewish teacher, if he could have consented to say anything to Mohammed about Jesus, must have ridiculed and vilified him. "Hätte jüdischer Einfluss auf Mohammed bestimmend eingewirkt, so hätte er entweder über Jesus schweigen oder ihn beschimpfen müssen. Palästinische Rabbinen, die in völlig christianisierten Städten wohnten, brachten es fertig, über Jesus völlig zu schweigen—das Schweigen des Hasses und der schimpflichen Nichtachtung; und der Talmud redet in den dürftigen Stellen, an den er auf Jesus zu sprechen kommt, nur mit beschimpfenden Worten von ihm." This, I think, hardly deals fairly with the Jews, nor sees clearly what sort of teaching was natural—one might even say necessary—under the circumstances now before us. The customary "Schweigen" in Jewish works written in Christian cities was a matter of course, and the attitude of the Talmud is also perfectly defensible. On the other hand, there was never lack of Jews, all through the Middle Ages, who spoke appreciatingly of Jesus, while rejecting the Christian dogmas. In the present case, whatever the teacher's preference may have been, Mohammed's own intention must have been the deciding factor. He knew the Jews to be a minority, and on the other hand was profoundly conscious of the religion of the Abyssinians and of the great Christian empire whose center was at Byzantium.[33] He was bound to make Christian allies, not enemies. Any vilification of Jesus would have led him to reject his teacher as untrustworthy. The latter of course knew this, and took care to keep the teaching in his own hands. There was certainly reason to fear what a Christian would teach in regard to the Jews. Now that the time had come for Mohammed to ask, from one who

[33] [See Lammens, L'Arabie Occidentale avant l'Hégire, p. 80, top].

evidently knew: "What does the 'Book' of the Christians tell about 'Īsā ibn Maryam?" the answer was given in good faith, *as far as it went*. That which Mohammed already knew was confirmed and supplemented, and numerous interesting details, chiefly from folklore, were added. The informant was certainly acquainted with the Gospels, but no particle of gospel information concerning the grown man Jesus, or his reported lineage, or his activities (excepting that, as Mohammed must already have heard, he performed miracles), or his teaching, or his followers, was given forth. The doctrine of the Virgin Birth, the most prominent of all the Christian shibboleths at that time, could be acquiesced in—it cost nothing; and it could not possibly have been combated!

What, according to the Koran, was the mission of Jesus? Numerous passages give the same vague answer: He was sent to confirm the Israelites in the true doctrine, in the teachings of the Torah (3:43 f.; 5:50; 43:63 f.; 57:27; 61:6), to insist on the worship of only one God (5:76), to warn against straying from the faith of Abraham and Moses and forming new sects (42:11)! It is very difficult to believe that any one of the verses here cited could have been written by Mohammed if he had ever talked with a Christian, orthodox or heretical; but they contain exactly what he would have acquired from the teaching which I am supposing. He knew that the followers of Jesus had ultimately chosen to form a separate sect, and that Jews and Christians were in controversy, each party declaring the other to be mistaken (2:107); but *why* the new sect had been formed, he did not at all know. He says in 3:44 that Jesus "made lawful" some things which had been prohibited. This may have been given him by his teacher, or it may be the reflection of his own doctrine (useful for his legislation), that some foods were forbidden the Israelites in punishment for their sins; see 4:158 and 3:87.

The passage 19:1–15 is of great importance as evidence of the source of Mohammed's information in regard to the prophet 'Īsā. Here is an extended *literary* connection with the Christian scriptures, the one and only excerpt from the New Testament, namely an abridgment of Luke 1:5–25, 57–66. This was discussed in the Second Lecture, and the details need not be repeated here. The account of the aged and upright Hebrew

priest and the birth of his son in answer to prayer, reading like a bit of
Old Testament history, would appeal to any Israelite of literary tastes as
interesting—and harmless. But as soon as the account of the birth of
Jesus is reached, the gospel narrative is dropped as though it were red-
hot, and Mohammed is left to flounder on alone, knowing only the bare
fact that John was the kinsman and forerunner of Jesus, and the dogma
of the Virgin Birth; things which his people had long ago learned,
especially from the Abyssinians. It seems possible to draw two conclusions with certainty: *first,* Mohammed was told the story of Zachariah
and John by a learned man; and *second,* the man was by no means a
Christian.

Horovitz, p. 129, declares that he can see no Jewish influence in the
Koranic utterances regarding Jesus. It may, however, be possible to recognize such influence from what is withheld, as well as from what is said.
The instructor, in this case, certainly knew what was told about Jesus in
the Four Gospels; but not a word of it came to the ear of Mohammed.
On the contrary, the bits of personal and family history of Jesus which
appear in the Koran are all derived from fanciful tales which were in
popular circulation; tales which a literary rabbi would certainly have
known, and which, from his point of view, were perfectly harmless. We
at the present day have some knowledge of them from surviving fragments of the "apocryphal gospel" literature. See, in the Koran, 3:32, 39,
43, and 5:110. The nature of the teaching with which Mohammed had
been supplied appears most clearly in the Suras (especially 3, 4, and 5)
revealed at Medina, during the time when the attitude of the prophet
toward the Jews was one of bitter hostility. It is evident that he then tried
to make much of Jesus and his history and his importance as a prophet,
and to remember all that he could of what he had formerly been told; but
what he had at his command was next to nothing. Any arguments or
accusations that he could have used against the Jews he would have been
certain to employ, and any Christian, lettered or unlettered, would have
supplied him with plenty of material; but he had in fact no ammunition
beyond what the Jews' own tradition had given him. In one very late
utterance, 5:85, he makes a valiant attempt to put the Christians high

above the Jews: the latter are the chief enemies of Islam, the former are its greatest friends. But he very unwisely attempts to tell wherein the excellence of the Christians consists, and can only specify their priests and monks—of whom recently (in 57:27) he had expressed a low opinion!

Mohammed did not know that 'Īsā had met with opposition from his people other than that which his predecessors had endured, and this is most significant. If he had known the fact, he could not have failed to make use of it; but it had not been told him. It was a mere matter of course that 'Īsā's contemporaries tried to kill him; the Hebrew people had been wont to kill their prophets (2:81, 85), as their own scriptures and popular traditions declared (see the Strack-Billerbeck comment on Matt. 23:35-37). That any special significance had been attached, by the Christians or others, to the death of 'Īsā, or to his ascension, Mohammed never had heard. For the docetic doctrine which he gives forth (4:156), asserting that it was not Jesus who was executed, but another who was miraculously substituted for him, it is quite superfluous to search for a heretical Christian or Manichaean (!) source. The heresy was old, and very widely known, though of course rarely adopted. *It precisely suited the purpose of Mohammed's Jewish instructor.* 'Īsā, thus escaping the fate intended for him, was taken up to heaven (3:48), as numerous others had been taken. No Christian doctrine was more universally held and built upon than *the Second Coming.* The Arabian prophet could easily have fitted it into his scheme of things, if he had known of it; at least to the extent of giving the Christian prophet some such important place in the Day of Judgment as he holds in the later Muslim eschatology; but there is nothing of the sort in the Koran.

The conclusion to be drawn from all this is evident, and certain: Mohammed derived his main impression of the prophet " 'Īsā" and his work from Jewish teaching, very shrewdly given.

In support of this conclusion a word may be added in regard to the various indications of Christian influence which some have claimed to find in the Koran, especially in recent years. Nöldeke's pioneer work, his *Geschichte des Qorāns* (1860), recognized hardly any Christian element. He declared (p. 2): "Gewiss sind die besten Theile des Islāms

jüdischen Ursprungs"; and again (p. 5): "Die Hauptquelle der Offen-
barungen . . . . bildeten für Muhhammed die Juden. . . . . Viel geringer
ist dagegen der Einfluss des Christenthums auf den Qorān." On the contrary, in Schwally's revision of this work we are given the impression of
a strong Christian element in Islam at its very beginning. We read (p. 8)
that in numerous particulars the influence of Christianity is "beyond any
doubt" (ausser allem Zweifel), and the following are specified: the in-
stitution of vigils; [34] some forms of the prayer-ritual; the use of the
"Christian" term *furqān* "to mean revelation"; the central significance of
the conception of the Last Day; and the superiority assigned to Jesus
above all the prophets. The conclusion is (*ibid.*), that "Islam might be
regarded as the form in which Christianity made its way into all Arabia."

The items in the above list are all taken over from Wellhausen, *Reste*
(1887), 205–209, and have been repeated by others, e. g. by Rudolph, p. 63.
Each one of these claims is considered elsewhere in the present Lectures, and
it will suffice to say here that *not a single one of them is valid*. The conclusion expressed seventy years ago by Muir in his *Life of Mahomet*, II,
289, is still very near the truth if it is limited to Mohammed and the
Koran: "We do not find a single ceremony or doctrine of Islam in the
smallest degree moulded, or even tinged, by the peculiar tenets of Christianity." [35]

Ibrāhīm and Ismā'īl. The importance of these two patriarchs in the
genesis of Islam has not been duly appreciated. We must first bear in
mind the ethnic relationship which gave such encouragement to Mo-

[34] [This refers to the prophet's admonition to pray and (especially) recite the Koran *at
night*—probably the only time when the most of his converts had opportunity to learn the
ritual prescribed for them. (The nocturnal prayer was soon superseded, as no longer necessary, by the increased number of daily prayers; see the Fifth Lecture.) The need of private
devotions in the night season was always felt by the especially devout in Israel, from the
Psalter onwards; and even public services at certain times were the rule in some medieval
Jewish communities, as at Qairawan in the time of Hai Gaon (I owe this reference to Professor Obermann). In *Berachoth* 14a (bottom) the devotee who spends the night reading the
Torah is commended. Mohammed had seen something of the sort at Mekka; see Sura 3:109,
mentioned in the preceding Lecture. On the general subject of Jewish asceticism, see now especially Montgomery, "Ascetic Strains in Early Judaism," J. B. L., vol. 51 (1932), pp. 183–
213].

[35] [Probably the fast of Ramadan should be excepted, but even this is by no means certain].

hammed in his wish to consort with the Jews and his attempt to gain
their support. The Arabs were Ishmaelites, according to the Hebrew tradition. God said to Abraham (Gen. 17, 20): "As for Ishmael, I have heard
thee; behold, I have blessed him, and will make him fruitful, and will
multiply him exceedingly; twelve princes shall he beget, and I will make
him a great nation." The twelve princes, subsequently named (25, 13 ff.),
represent Arabian tribes or districts; notice especially Kedar, Duma
(Dūmat al-Jandal), and Teimā. The "great nation" is the people of
Arabia. Ishmael was circumcised (17, 26), was with his father at the time
of his death, and assisted Isaac in burying him (25, 9). The Arabs were
rightful heirs of the religion of their father Abraham, though they chose
paganism instead.

On this foundation Mohammed built his tales of Abraham and Ishmael
at Mekka. In the 14th Sura, which bears the title 'Abraham,' he introduces, in a characteristically casual and obscure manner, his association
of Ishmael with the Ka'ba. I say "his association," but it is quite likely that
he himself did not originate the idea. The Arabs cannot possibly have
remained ignorant of the fact that the Hebrew scriptures declared Abraham and Ishmael to be their ancestors. It was then most natural that they
should have been associated, in popular tradition, with the ancient sanctuary. In verses 38–42 we read: "Remember the time when Abraham said,
Lord, make this land [36] secure, and restrain me and my children from
worshipping idols. Lord, they have led astray many men; whoever then
follows me, is mine; and if any disobey me—thou art forgiving and
merciful." (Here he refers to the children of Ishmael, the unbelieving
Arabs.) "O our Lord, I have caused some of my offspring to settle in an
unfruitful valley, at the site of thy holy house; thus, Lord, in order that
they may offer prayer. Grant therefore that the hearts of some men may
be inclined toward them; and provide them with the fruits of the earth,
that they perchance may be grateful. . . . . Praise to God, who gave me,
even in old age, Ishmael and Isaac; verily my Lord is one who hears
prayer."

This passage, together with the majority of those which mention Ish-

[36] [That is, the Hijaz].

mael, I should assign to the prophet's later Mekkan period. (This is not, however, a generally accepted conclusion, as will presently appear.) In general, Mohammed has very little to say about Ishmael; and there was good reason for his reticence. He did not himself read the Old Testament, but merely built upon what he had been told. The episode of Hagar was of no value for his purposes; in fact, he never mentions Hagar at all.[37] The early Jewish narrators seem to have felt little interest in the disinherited elder son of Abraham, and left him at one side.

After Islam had become a great power in the world, new light dawned, and the story-tellers, both Jewish and Mohammedan, found that they knew more about Ishmael and his family. An early example is the picturesque tale, found in the Jerusalem Targum and apparently alluded to in the Pirqē Rabbi Eliezer, of Ishmael's two wives, so very different in character and disposition; and of the visits of the "very old man" Abraham to the tent of his nomad son, far away in the Arabian desert. The names of the two wives (otherwise "tent-pins"), Ayesha and Fatima, make it quite certain that this legend was not known to Mohammed and his contemporaries.

The famous well, Zemzem, at Mekka is also brought into connection with the Biblical history. According to Pirqē Abōth, one of the ten things created בֵּין הַשְּׁמָשׁוֹת, that is, between the sixth day of creation and the following day of rest, was "the mouth of the well." This refers, as all interpreters agree, to the miraculously traveling well of the Israelites ("the spiritual rock that followed them," 1 Corinthians 10, 4), mentioned in Ex. 17 and Num. 20 and 21, in the account of the journey from Egypt to the promised land. Here again the Jerusalem Targum and the Pirqē Rabbī Eliezer bring in the story of Ishmael, by including also the well which appeared to Hagar (Gen. 21, 19). The Mohammedan orthodox Tradition (ḥadīth) then puts the capstone on all this by making Zemzem the well which saved the lives of Hagar and her son.[38] This, to be sure, would mean that the mother and child had walked some 600 miles on

---

[37] [The orthodox Mohammedan tradition supplies this lack, to be sure. See for instance Krehl's Boḵhari II, 78, below].

[38] [Boḵhārī, ed. Krehl, II, 78 below].

the occasion described. Such sages as Abu Huraira and Ibn 'Abbās were not troubled by considerations of geography; and inasmuch as this improvement of the legend is early Muslim tradition, it might be termed a doctrine of primitive Islam. But Mohammed knew better; at least, he says not a word in the Koran about the sacred well at Mekka.

The highly significant passage in which Abraham and Ishmael are associated in the founding of the Ka'ba at Mekka is 2, 118–123. "When his Lord tested Abraham with certain commands, which he fulfilled, he said, I make thee an example for mankind to follow. Abraham said, And those of my posterity? God answered, My compact does not include the evil-doers." This refers to the pagan Arabs, the descendants of Ishmael; like the verse 14:39, already cited. The passage proceeds: "Remember the time when we made the house [that is, the Ka'ba] a place of resort and of security for mankind, and said, Take the 'station of Abraham' (also 3:91) as a place of prayer; and how we laid upon Abraham and Ishmael the covenant obligation, saying, Make my house holy (cf. 80:14 and 98:2) for those who make the circuit, for those who linger in it, those who bow down, and prostrate themselves in devotion. And when Abraham said, Lord, make this land secure, and nourish its people with the fruits of the earth; those among them who believe in God and the last day; he answered, As for him who is unbelieving, I will provide him with little; and thereafter I will drive him to the punishment of hell-fire; it will be an evil journey" (a warning to the men of Mekka, and to all the Arabs, the faithless Ishmaelites).

Then comes the important statement regarding the founding of the Ka'ba; important, because it plainly contradicts the orthodox Muslim tradition. "And when Abraham with Ishmael was raising the foundations of the house, he said, Lord, accept this from us; . . . . make us submissive to thee, and make of our offspring a nation submissive to thee; and declare to us our ritual. . . . . Lord, send also among them a messenger of their own, who shall recite to them thy signs and teach them the book and divine wisdom, and purify them; verily thou art the mighty and wise." According to the later Muslim doctrine, the Ka'ba was first built by Adam; the station (or standing place) of Abraham is the spot inside the sanctuary where his footprint in the rock is still to be seen; the command to the two patriarchs, "Make my house clean," meant "Cleanse it of idols." But the meaning of the Koran is plain, that the holy station and the holy house began with Abraham and his son.

In the verses which immediately follow, it is expressly said that the true and final religion, Islām, was first revealed to the family of the patriarch. Verse 126: "Abraham and Jacob gave this command to their sons: God has chosen for you the (true) religion; you must not die without becoming Muslims." We could wish to know how important in Mohammed's thought this conception of the genesis of Islam was, and how early it was formed in his mind. I shall try to answer the question at the close of this Lecture.

In so far as we are reduced to conjecture, there are certain known factors in the Mekkan prophet's religious development that would lead us to suppose, if nothing should hinder the supposition, that he attached himself very early and very firmly to Abraham's family when he sought (as he must have sought) support in the past for the faith which he set himself to proclaim. We have seen how essential to all his thinking, from the very first, was the idea of the written revelation, the scriptural guidance given by God to men. Jews and Christians alike were "people of the Book"; in each case a book of divine origin. But Jews and Christians were in sharpest disagreement. As the Koran puts it in Sura 2, 107, and as Mohammed had known long before he began his public ministry, "The Jews say, The Christians are all wrong (lit., rest on nothing); and the Christians say, The Jews are all wrong; and yet they read the scriptures!" Now Mohammed knew that these two religions were branches from the same stock; that the Christian sect had its beginnings in Judaism; and that the Christians held to the Hebrew scriptures, and claimed for themselves the prophets and patriarchs. The Hebrew people were the children of Abraham; so also, then, were the Christians, even though they attached no importance to this origin. Did not these facts point clearly to the starting point of the *final* religion? Here also the Arabs, the sons of Ishmael, came in for their long-lost inheritance. Mohammed could only conclude that Jews and Christian alike had been led away from the truth.

The right way was now to be shown to them, as well as to the Arabs. This belief he expresses at first confidently, at length bitterly, at last fiercely.

It is not always easy to determine, from the Koran, either the relative age or the relative importance of Mohammed's leading ideas. We have seen the reasons for this. On this very point, the place occupied by the Hebrew. patriarchs in the development of the prophet's religious doctrine, there has been some difference of opinion.

According to early Muslim tradition, there were in Arabia, not only in Mekka and Medina but also in a few other cities, before the time of Mohammed's public appearance as a prophet, certain seekers after truth, who revolted against the Arabian idolatry. They called themselves *ḥanīfs,* and professed to seek "the religion of Abraham," their ancestor. Now Mohammed in the Koran repeatedly applies to Abraham the term *ḥanīf* as descriptive of his religion. Where and how he got possession of the term cannot be declared with certainty, but may be conjectured, as we have seen. Certainly it came originally from the Hebrew חנף *ḥānēf;* and probably its employment by him as a term of praise, rather than of reproach, indicates that in his mind it designated one who *"turned away"* from the surrounding paganism. Be that as it may, his use of the word seemed to give support to the tradition just mentioned, until a thorough investigation of the latter showed it to be destitute of any real foundation.

The conclusive demonstration was furnished by Snouck Hurgronje, in his brilliant and searching monograph entitled *Het Mekkaansche Feest* (1880). Snouck made it clear to all who study his argument that Mohammed himself had no knowledge of any Arabian "hanīfs," and that the tradition had its origin in a theory of later growth. The conclusion at which he arrived went still farther than this, however, for he denied that the prophet had any special interest in the Hebrew patriarchs in the earlier part of his career. This is a matter which seems to me to be in need of further investigation.

Sprenger, *Das Leben und die Lehre des Mohammad,* Vol. II (1862), pp. 276-285, gave at some length his reasons for believing that Mohammed himself invented the association of Abraham with the Ka'ba, that he for some time supposed Jacob to be the son of Abraham, that he learned of Ishmael's parentage only at a comparatively late date, etc.; all this very loosely reasoned, and arbitrary in its treatment of the Koran. Snouck, starting out from the plausible portion of Sprenger's argument, developed thoroughly and consistently the theory that the prophet's especial interest in the Hebrew patriarchs arose in Medina, as a result of his failure to gain the support of the Jews. That is, in his reaction against the religion of Moses (?) he turned back to those earlier prophets to whose family he could claim to belong. Accordingly, after removing to Yathrib and suffering his great disappointment there, he began to make great use of the two patriarchs Abraham and Ishmael, to whom while in Mekka he had attached no especial importance.

The complete argument will be found in the reprint of Snouck's *Mekkaansche Feest* in his *Verspreide Geschriften*, I, 22–29; repeated also by him in the *Revue de l'histoire des religions*, vol. 30 (1894), pp. 64 ff. His principal contentions are the following: (1) In the Mekkan Surås Abraham is merely one among many prophets, not a central figure. (2) The phrase *millat Ibrāhīm*, "the religion of Abraham," as the designation of Islam, is peculiar to the Medina Suras of the Koran. (3) It was only after leaving Mekka that Mohammed conceived the idea of connecting Abraham and Ishmael with the Ka'ba. (4) In several comparatively late Mekkan Suras the prophet declares that before his time "no warner" had been sent to the Arabs (32:2; 34:43; 36:5). Yet at this same time Ishmael is said by him to have "preached to his people" (19:55 f.). Does not this show that the prophet while in Mekka had not associated Ishmael with the Arabs?

These conclusions are accepted, as proven, in the Nöldeke-Schwally *Geschichte des Qorāns* (see especially pp. 146 f., 152), and have been widely adopted. I think, however, that the argument will not bear close examination, in the light of present-day estimates of the Arabian prophet's equipment. Mohammed's knowledge of Hebrew-Jewish lore in general, and of the Pentateuchal narratives in particular, is appraised considerably higher now than it was in 1880, and this is true also of Arabian culture in the Hijaz. Whether or not the Mekkan Arabs had known that the

Hebrew patriarch Ishmael was their ancestor, Mohammed must have
known it and have been profoundly impressed by the fact, very early in
his course of instruction. The Koran, as I shall endeavor to show, testifies
clearly to this effect. Mohammed certainly could not cut loose from the
Jews by adopting Abraham! If he had wished to "emancipate Islam from
Judaism," *and had found himself free to make his own choice,* he could
easily and successfully have denied the Ishmaelite origin of the Arabs,
falsely reported by the Jews. The founding of the Ka'ba could equally
well have been ascribed to Noah, or "Idrīs," or some other ancient worthy.
There is not a particle of evidence to show that the Koran gave less
weight in Medina to Moses and his ordinances than had been given in
Mekka. The fact is just the contrary; and the prophet not only leans
heavily on Moses, but openly professes to do so (e.g. in 5:48 f.!). And
finally, Snouck's theory is not supported by the Koran unless the text of
the latter is reconstructed by the excision and removal from Mekkan con-
texts of certain passages which, as they stand, would be fatal to the argument.

In reply to the principal contentions listed above: (1) In one of the
very early Mekkan Suras Abraham is emphatically a "central figure" in
the history of the world. In the closing verses of Sura 87 we read of "the
primal books, *the books of Abraham and Moses.*" Whatever the prophet's
idea may have been as to the contents of these "books," Abraham is here
made *the father of the written revelation of God to mankind.* He instituted "The Book," of which Mohammed stood in such awe. In another
early Sura, 53, these "books" are again mentioned, and in the same connection Abraham is characterized in a significant way; vs. 38, "(the book)
of Abraham, *who paid in full.*" This last phrase is elucidated in 2:118,
where it is said: "When his Lord tested Abraham with certain commands, which he fulfilled, he said, 'I make thee an example for mankind.'" The command to the patriarch to sacrifice his own son is of
course the one especially in mind, and it is plain that Mohammed had
essentially the same idea of Abraham in the two passages.

The account of the attempted sacrifice which the Koran gives, in
37:99–113, is important for our knowledge of Mohammed's attitude

toward the Jews in the early part of his career at Mekka. Abraham is given tidings of the coming birth of his "mild son" [39] (vs. 99). The boy grows up, and is rescued from the sacrificial knife by divine intervention (vss. 103–107). *Thereafter* (vs. 112), *the birth of Isaac is foretold to Abraham.* This seemed to Snouck (pp. 23 f.) to show that Mohammed had become confused and uncertain in regard to the story—unless vss. 112 f. could be regarded as an interpolation. But the prophet, far from being confused, shows here both his acquaintance with the Old Testament narrative and also his practical wisdom. Why does he not *name* the elder son? The answer is plain. Mohammed was perfectly aware, even before he began preaching in public, that Abraham's first-born son, Ishmael, was the father of the Arabs. In the Hebrew narrative he is an utterly insignificant figure, an unworthy son of the great religious founder. The Arabian prophet, instituting a religion centering in Arabia, saw his opportunity to improve this state of things. It is very significant that he employs three verses of his very brief narrative (101–103) to show that Abraham's son was informed beforehand of the intended sacrifice *and fully acquiesced in it*—a most important touch which has no counterpart in the Biblical story. Ishmael was a true "muslim." He leaves out the name, but this is not all. The mention of Isaac is introduced *after* the concluding formula (vss. 109–111) which runs through the chapter, and without any adverb of time (such as *thumma*); and thus he completely avoids unnecessary trouble either with the Jews who were his instructors or with his own few followers. The whole passage is a monument to his shrewd foresight, a quality which we are liable constantly to underestimate in studying his method of dealing with the Biblical narratives.

(2) As for the *millat Ibrāhīm*, "the religion of Abraham," the single passage 12:38, of the Mekkan period, is sufficient to nullify the argument. Could any one suppose that Mohammed meant by the *milla* of Abraham, Isaac, Jacob, and Joseph any other religion than Islam? Ishmael could not have been mentioned here, since Joseph is enumerating his own ancestors. More than this, there are two other Mekkan passages (16:124 and 22:77)

[39] [*Too* mild, as the event proved, to make his own children follow the right way!].

in which the phrase *millat Ibrāhīm* occurs. These shall receive further notice presently.

(3) I have already expressed the opinion that the association of Abraham and Ishmael with the sanctuary at Mekka is pre-Islamic (see also Schwally, 147, note 3). As for Mohammed himself, he sets forth the doctrine fully in Sura 14:38-42. The whole chapter is Mekkan, and has always been so classed; and there is no imaginable reason why an interpolation should have been made at this point. Yet Schwally, p. 152, cuts out these verses from the Sura on the sole ground that Snouck's theory requires their excision. The latter treats the passage, on p. 29, quite arbitrarily. It is obvious why the patriarch here names Ishmael and Isaac, not Isaac and Jacob. Verse 37 had just spoken of the countless favors of Allah, who *"gives you some portion of all that you ask of him."* This introduces the mention of Abraham, who in vs. 41 praises Allah for giving him *two sons* in his old age, and adds, "verily my Lord is the hearer of prayer!" Could any one ask for a better connection? The verses are Mekkan, and always occupied this place in the Sura.

(4) The passages which mention the "warner" give no aid whatever to the theory. The prophet would at all times have maintained that the Arabian peoples had never had a "messenger" sent to them. The only passage in which there is mention of admonition given by Ishmael is 19:56, where it is said that he commanded "his family" (this, unquestionably, is what *ahlahu* means) to pray and give alms. As "a prophet and messenger" he must have done this much. But it is made perfectly plain in the Koran—the principal passages have already been discussed —that his children paid no attention to the admonition. Long before Arabia began to be peopled with the Ishmaelite tribes, the disobedient sons had passed away, along with the instruction given to them. No Arabian tribe had ever heard a word in regard to the true religion.

The Question of Composite Mekkan Suras. Some brief space must be given here to a matter which really calls for a monograph. A moment ago, I claimed as Mekkan utterances of the prophet two passages (16:124

and 22:77) which by occidental scholars are now quite generally regarded
as belonging to the Medina period. The 16th Sura is Mekkan, as no one
doubts. Of its 128 verses, Schwally assigns 43, 44, and 111–125 to Medina;
at the same time combating, on obviously sufficient grounds, the opinions
of those who would assign to Medina numerous other passages. In regard
to Sura 22 Nöldeke had declared (p. 158), that "the greater part of it"
was uttered at Mekka, but that its most significant material came from the
Medina period. It accordingly is now classed as a Medina Sura in the
standard treatises and in Rodwell's Koran; see also Nicholson's *Literary
History of the Arabs,* p. 174. In the course of the argument concerning the
association of Abraham and Ishmael with the Ka'ba I discussed a supposed insertion in Sura 14, with the result of showing that the theory of
interpolation is at least quite unnecessary. These are merely single examples out of a multitude. The accepted working hypothesis as to the
composition of the Koran recognizes a considerable revision, after the
Hijra, of the later Mekkan Suras by the insertion of longer or shorter
passages, which certain criteria enable us to detect. Of course the theory
has its apparent justification; the question is, whether it has not run wild.

The Koran is a true *corpus vile,* no one cares how much it is chopped
up. The Arabs themselves have been the worst choppers. Their ancient
theory of the sacred book led to just this treatment. It was miraculously
revealed, and miraculously preserved. Mohammed, being "unable to read
and write," left no copy behind at his death; so when it became necessary
to make a standard volume, its various portions were collected "from
scraps of paper, parchment, and leather, from palm-leaves, tablets of
wood, bones, stones, and from the breasts of men." This is
something like Ezra's restoration, from memory, of the lost Hebrew scriptures, twenty-four canonical and seventy apocryphal books
(4 Ezra, 14:44 ff.), and the two accounts are of like value for historical
purposes. The Muslim commentators found no difficulty in seeing—as
they did see—oracles of Mekka and Medina wonderfully jumbled together in many Suras. Their analysis of the chapters which they themselves pronounced Mekkan was based either on fancied historical allusions
or on fundamentally mistaken notions as to the activities and associations

of the prophet in the years before the Hijra. The disagreement of these early interpreters, moreover, was very wide.

Mohammed himself wrote down the successive Suras; and he gave them out as complete units, a fact which is especially obvious in such a group as the *Ḥā-Mīm* chapters, 40–46, but is hardly less evident throughout the book. It might also be inferred from the challenge to his critics to produce "ten Suras," in 11:16. He had his amanuenses, who made some copies for distribution. He himself supplemented a number of the completed Suras, after they had been for some time in circulation, making important insertions or additions, obviously needed, and generally indicated as secondary by their form. Thus, 73:20 is an easily recognizable Medina appendage to a Mekkan Sura. The cautious addition in regard to Jesus in the 19th Sura (vss. 35–41, marked off from their context by the rhyme) is another well known example. In 74:30, the prophet's "nineteen angels" (numbered for the sake of the rhyme) called forth some ridicule, which he thereafter rebuked in a lengthy insertion, quite distinct in form from the rest of the chapter.[40] In such cases it certainly is the most plausible supposition that Mohammed made the alteration in writing, with his own hand.

It might at the outset seem a plausible hypothesis that the prophet would make numerous alterations, in the course of time, in the Suras which he had composed, as his point of view changed and new interests came into the foreground. The loose structure of the Koran in nearly all of its longer chapters rendered interpolation singularly easy. The kaleidoscope is constantly turning, and the thought leaps from one subject to another, often without any obvious connection. Since the verses are separate units, each with its rhymed ending (often a mere stock phrase), nothing could be easier than to insert new verses in order to supplement, or explain, or qualify; or even in order to correct and replace an objectionable utterance, as was done (according to an old tradition) in the middle of the 53rd Sura. It is important to note, however, that we should not be able to recognize any such insertions, unless the prophet called attention

---

40 [In the oriental texts of the Koran this forms a single verse. In Fluegel's edition it occupies vss. 31–34, as far as the word *huwa*].

to them in some striking way. Did Mohammed, in fact, freely *revise* his
(i. e. Gabriel's) revelations? There is a doctrine clearly stated by him, and
well illustrated, that certain utterances are "annulled" by subsequent outgivings. The latter, however, are never put beside the former, nor given
specific reference to them, but merely make their appearance wherever
it may happen—that is, when and where Gabriel found the new teaching
desirable. In like manner, the supposed insertions now under discussion,
"Medina additions to Mekkan Suras," are as a rule given no obvious motive by anything in their context, but seem purely fortuitous. If they
really are insertions, and were made by the prophet, it was not with any
recognizable purpose.

For one reason in particular it is not easy to suppose any considerable
amount of alteration in the divine oracles, after they had once been
finished and made public. From the first they were learned by heart and
constantly recited by those who had committed them to memory. As early
as Sura 73:1-6 the prophet urges his followers to spend a part of the
night in reciting what they have learned, and it is implied that the
amount is already considerable. The acquisition was very easy, and before
the prophet's death the number of those who could repeat the whole
book without missing a word cannot have been very small. Under these
circumstances, any alteration, especially if made without apparent reason,
could not fail to be very disturbing. The few which (as we have seen)
the prophet himself made were doubtless explained by him; and we
may be sure that he would have permitted no other to change the divine
messages! After his death, the precise form of words was jealously
guarded; and when, through the unforeseen but inevitable accidents of
wider transmission, variant readings crept in, so that copies in different
cities showed some real disagreement, a standard text was made, probably differing only in unimportant details from the form originally given
out by Mohammed. In the early subsequent history, indeed, minor variations in the text, consisting mainly of interesting differences of orthography
and peculiarities of grammatical usage, amounted to a large number; see
the very important chapter on the history of the text in Nöldeke's

Geschichte des Qorāns. But whoever reads the Koran through must feel that we have the prophet before us in every verse.

The *dating* of the Suras of the Koran, as of Mekka or Medina, is generally, though not always, an easy matter. Any chapter of considerable length is sure to contain evidence clearly indicating the one city or the other as the place of its origin. The simple classification of this nature which was made by the best of the early Mohammedan scholars is nearly everywhere confirmed by modern critics. Even in the case of the briefer Suras there is not often room for doubt. The possibility of dating more exactly, however, is soon limited. The career of the prophet in Medina, covering ten years, is well known to us in its main outlines. Since a number of important events, chronologically fixed, are plainly referred to in the Koran, about one-half of the twenty or more Medina Suras can be approximately located. Not so with the twelve years of the Mekkan revelations. Here, there is an almost complete lack of fixed points, and we have very inadequate information as to Mohammed's personal history and the development of his ideas and plans. It is possible to set apart, with practical certainty on various grounds, a considerable number of Suras as *early;* and a much smaller number can be recognized with almost equal certainty as coming from the last years of the Mekkan period. Between the arbitrary limits of these two groups a certain development, partly in the literary form and partly in the relative emphasis given to certain doctrines, can be traced in the remaining Suras; but with no such distinctness as to make possible a chronological arrangement. This is true of all three of the conventional "Mekkan periods."

The native interpreters, as already observed, analyzed the Mekkan Suras to their heart's content; recognizing allusions to very many persons, events, and circumstances, and accordingly treating this or that Sura without regard to considerations of literary or chronological unity. Modern occidental scholars saw that these hypotheses as to actors and scenes were generally either purely fanciful or else plainly mistaken; in Nöldeke's treatise, for example, they meet with wholesale rejection. The underlying theory, that of casually composite chapters, in which oracles from widely different periods might stand side by side without apparent reason for their proximity, was nevertheless adopted. The criteria employed by the Muslim scholars in identifying Medina verses in Mekkan Suras were also, in considerable part, taken over as valid. These consist of single words and phrases, often arbitrarily interpreted, and also of allusions to conditions supposed to be characteristic of the Medina period but not of the earlier time.

Here the critic is on slippery ground. That which Mohammed gave forth from time to time was largely determined by the immediate circumstances, concerning which it is likely to be the case that we either are not informed at all, or else are wrongly informed by the guesses of the native commentators. Ideas which (in the nature of the case) must have been in the prophet's mind from the very beginning may happen to find their chief expression only at a late date. Certain evils existed for some time before they became very serious. There were "hypocrites" in Mekka as well as in Medina. Such words as "strive," "contend," and "victory" gained great significance after the battle of Bedr; but they ought not to be forbidden to the prophet's Mekkan vocabulary. In Sura 29, for example, which unquestionably in the main was uttered before the Hijra, many of the Muslim authorities assign the first ten verses to Medina, and Nöldeke follows them.[41] Verse 45 is similarly treated—in spite of 6:153, 16:126, and 23:98! In fact, there is no valid reason for such analysis; the whole Sura is certainly Mekkan, and so not a few scholars, oriental and occidental, have decided. Another example of the forced interpretation of single words is to be seen in the treatment of the very brief Sura 110. If Mohammed believed himself to be a prophet, and had faith in the ultimate triumph of the religion which he proclaimed, it is far easier to suppose that this little outburst came from the time when he first met with serious opposition than to imagine it delivered late in the Medina period, as is now commonly done. The word "victory" is no more remarkable here than it is in the closing verses of Sura 32.

Another mistake made by the early commentators has had serious con-

---

[41] [Here, as in the following examples, I refer to the Nöldeke-Schwally *Geschichte,* as the standard and by far the most influential work].

sequences. Having little or no knowledge of the presence of Jews in Mekka, and with their eyes always on the important Jewish tribes of Medina and the prophet's dealings with them, they habitually assigned to the Medina period the allusions to Jewish affairs which they found in Mekkan Suras; and in this they sometimes have been followed by modern scholars. It is one principal aim of the present Lectures to show that Mohammed's personal contact with the Jews was closer (as well as much longer continued) before the Hijra than after it. By far the most of what he learned of Israelite history, literature, customs, and law was acquired in Mekka. It is also a mistaken supposition that he met with no determined opposition from the Jews, resulting in bitter resentment on his part, before the Hijra.[42] On the contrary, he was perfectly aware, before leaving Mekka, that the Jews as a whole were against him, though some few gave him support. After the migration to Yathrib, when his cause seemed to triumph, he doubtless cherished the hope that now at length the Jews would acknowledge his claim; and when they failed to do so, his resentment became active hostility.

It is not difficult to see why the Muslim historians and commentators habitually assign to Medina those passages in the Koran in which Mohammed is given contact with Jewish affairs, in default of any definite allusion to Mekka as the scene. The latter city was the Muslim sanctuary *par excellence,* from the prophet's day onward, and unbelieving foreigners were not welcome. As for the Jews themselves, they of course realized, after seeing how their compatriots at Yathrib had been evicted or butchered, that Mekka was no place for them. Their exodus began during Mohammed's lifetime, and must soon have been extensive. After this emigration, their former influence in the holy city, as far as it was kept in memory, was at first minimized, and then ignored; eventually it was lost to sight. The prophet's close personal association with Mekkan Jews, and especially his debt to Jewish teachers (!), was of course totally unknown to the generations which later came upon the scene. On the other hand, they had very full knowledge of his continued contact with the

---

[42] [Hence the now customary assignment of Sura 98, plainly a Mekkan composition, to the Medina period].

Jews of Yathrib; and they very naturally interpreted the Koran in the light of this knowledge. Modern scholars have been far too easy-going in giving weight to these decisions of the native commentators, and the mistaken analysis of Mekkan Suras has too often been the result.

It would be fruitless to attempt to collect here the many "Medina" verses which have been found by Muslim scholars in the Mekkan chapters merely because of the mention of Jews. Some similar criticism may be found in Nöldeke-Schwally in the comments on 6:91, 7:156, and 29:45 (already mentioned), as well as in the passages about to be considered. It must be clear, from what has thus far been said, that the only sound and safe proceeding in the "higher criticism" of the Suras recognized as prevailingly Mekkan is to pronounce every verse in its original place unless there is absolute and unmistakable proof to the contrary. I know of no later additions to Mekkan Suras, with the exception of the few which Mohammed himself plainly indicated.[43]

All this has led up to the consideration of the two passages previously mentioned, 16:124 and 22:77, in which Islam is termed "the religion (*milla*) of Abraham." Both passages are now generally assigned to the Medina period, but for no valid reason. Both Suras are "in the main" Mekkan, as few would doubt. In Sura 16, verses 43 f. and 111 would naturally be supposed to refer to the migration to Abyssinia. Since however the latter verse speaks of "striving," an allusion to the holy war is postulated, and all three verses are referred to the Hijra; but the third stem of *jahada* was well known even in Mekka! Verse 119 is given to Medina on the ground that it probably refers to 6:147. If it does, this merely shows that 6 is earlier than 16; a conclusion which is opposed by no fact. Verse 125 is suspected of coming from Medina on the ground that "it deals with the Jewish sabbath." It is thus rendered natural (Schwally, p. 147) to assign the whole passage 111–125 to Medina; and

---

[43] [Interpolations and transpositions have often been postulated by interpreters of the Koran because of failure to take full account of Mohammed's very individual literary habits. Thus Nöldeke-Schwally, p. 144, will have the words: "So be not in doubt of meeting Him!" an interpolation, "da sie sich auf keine Weise in einen Zusammenhang bringen lassen." The words are thrown in as the summary of Moses' teaching; and those who heard the prophet *recite* the passage can have been in no doubt as to its meaning].

Abraham, in vs. 124, is accordingly counted out. But unless better evidence than the foregoing can be presented, the whole Sura must be pronounced Mekkan.

Sura 22 affords the best single illustration of the fact that the latest Mekkan revelations closely resemble those of Medina not only in style and vocabularly but also in some of the subjects which chiefly occupied the prophet's attention. Considerable portions are now declared to be later than the Hijra; see Nöldeke-Schwally, pp. 214 f. These shall be considered in as brief compass as possible.

Vs. 17 is by no means "a later insertion"; it has its perfect connection in the concluding words of the preceding verse. Vss. 25–38 give directions in regard to the rites of the *Ḥajj*, at the sacred house. Does this remove them from their Mekkan surroundings? Did not Mohammed (and his adherents) believe in the duty of the Pilgrimage before they migrated to Yathrib? Probably no one will doubt that they did so believe. It is very noticeable that the whole passage, as well as what precedes and follows it, is *argumentative;* addressed quite as plainly to the "idolaters" as to the Muslims. This is the tone of the whole Sura. Notice especially vss. 15 (and in Medina would certainly have been written: "Allah will help *his prophet*"); 32–36 (in the latter verse observe the words: "those who endure patiently what has befallen them"); 42–45; 48–50; 54–56; 66–71. In the last-named verse we see that the idolaters, among whom Mohammed is living and whom he is addressing, occasionally hear the Koran recited, and threaten to lay violent hands on those who recite it! The passage in regard to the *Ḥajj* is not mere prescription, for the instruction of the Muslims; it is designed to inform the Mekkans that Mohammed and his followers mean to observe the rites in the time-honored way, and that they have been unjustly debarred from the privilege. The prophet is thoroughly angry, and expresses himself in a way that shows that some sort of a *hijra* must soon be necessary. In vs. 40 formal permission is given to the Muslims to "fight because they have been wronged"; from which we may see what a pitch the Mekkans' persecution had reached. The description of the whole situation given in Ibn Hishām, 313 f., is generally convincing, as well as perfectly suited to this most interesting Sura.

The strongest support of the theory of later insertions in the chapter seemed to be given by vs. 57. Nöldeke saw here the mention of certain true believers, who after migrating from Mekka had been killed in battle; and he therefore of necessity pronounced the passage later than the battle of Bedr. The view that a general supposition was intended, rather than historical fact, seemed to him to be excluded by grammatical considerations. His footnote, repeated by Schwally, says: "If the reading were *man qutila,* 'if any one is killed,' then the verses could have been composed before the battle; but *alladhīna qutilū* excludes the conditional interpretation, and shows merely the completed action: 'those who were killed.'" It is evident that Nöldeke completely overlooked the passage 2:155 f., which is strikingly parallel in its wording, while fortunately there can be no difference of opinion as to the interpretation. In both cases we have merely a general hypothesis. Mohammed is not always bound by the rules of classical Arabic grammar (probably it would be more correct to say that his imagination was so vivid as to make the supposition an actual occurrence), and he frequently employs *alladhī* and *alladhīna* in exactly this way. The passage in our Sura refers to some lesser migration (or migrations) before the Hijra, and to Muslims who may die, or be killed, after this clear proof of their devotion to the cause of Allah. (Nothing is said of being killed *in battle*.)

Finally, vss. 76 ff. are said to have originated in Medina, because "they enjoin the holy war," and because of the mention of the "religion of Abraham." The interpretation of the first words of vs. 77 as referring to *the holy war* is not only unnecessary, however, but also seems out of keeping with what is said in the remainder of the verse. The believers are exhorted *to strive earnestly* for the true faith; compare the precisely similar use of this verb in the Mekkan passages 25:54 and 29:69. The saying in regard to Abraham is important for the history of the term "Islām," as will be seen. To conclude: Sura 22 is thoroughly homogeneous, containing *no* elements from the Medina period. And (as was said a moment ago) much stronger evidence than has thus far been offered must be produced before it can be maintained that Mekkan Suras were freely interpolated after the Hijra.

The Origin of the Term "Islām." The theory propounded by Professor Snouck Hurgronje and discussed in the preceding pages has, I think, helped to hide from sight the true source of the name which Mohammed gave to the faith of which he was the founder. The one thing which we usually can feel sure of knowing as to the origin of a great religion is how it got its name. In the case of "Islam," the only fact on which all scholars would agree is that the name was given by Mohammed. The formal title appears rather late in the Koran, but is virtually there very early, for the true believers are termed "Muslims" in the Suras of the first Mekkan period. There has been considerable difference of opinion as to what the word means. The great majority have always held that this verbal noun, *"islām,"* was chosen as meaning "submission"; that is, submission to the will of God; but not a few, especially in recent years, have sought another interpretation. It is not obvious why the prophet should have selected this name, nor does ordinary Arabic usage suggest this as the most natural meaning of the 4th stem of the very common verb *salima.*

Hence at least one noted scholar has proposed to understand the prophet's use of this verb-stem as conveying the idea of *coming into the condition of security* (Lidzbarski, in the *Zeitschrift für Semitistik,* I, 86). The meaning of "Islām" would then be "safety"; and in view of the long catalogue of unspeakable tortures in Gehenna which are promised to the unbelievers, this might seem an appealing title. The interpretation is far from convincing, however, in view of several passages in the Koran. Professor Margoliouth of Oxford, one of the foremost Arabists of our time, offered the theory that the Muslims were originally the adherents of the "false prophet" Musailima, who appeared in central Arabia at about the time of Mohammed. This theory, as might be expected, was not received with favor.

It has been doubted by some whether the term is really of Arabic origin; see Horovitz, *Untersuchungen,* p. 55; Nöldeke-Schwally, p. 20, note 2, and the references there given. The attempt to find a real equivalent in Aramaic or Syriac has failed, however; and I, for one, can see no good reason for doubting that we have here genuine native usage. Moreover, the only meaning of the term which suits all the Koranic passages is the one which has generally been adopted.

But why *"submission"*? This was never a prominently appearing feature of the Muslim's religion. It is not an attitude of mind characteristic of Mohammed himself. It is not a virtue especially dwelt upon in any part of the Koran. It would not in itself seem to be an attractive designation of the Arab's faith. Why was not the new religion named "Faith," or "Truth," or "Safety," or "Right-guidance," or "Striving," or "Victory"? —since these are ideas prominent in the Koran. Why "Submission"?

I believe that the origin of the name is to be found in a scene in the life of Abraham and Ishmael depicted in the Koran and already mentioned in this Lecture, and that the choice was made by Mohammed because of his doctrine that the final religion—or rather, the final form of the true religion—had its inception in the revelation given to Abraham and his family. The Koran knows of no "Muslims" prior to these patriarchs. We have seen that one of the very early Suras speaks of "the books of Moses and Abraham" (87:19). In another Sura of the same period we find the earliest occurrence of the designation "Muslims" (68:35). In what probably is the very last Mekkan utterance of the prophet (22:77), Abraham and the naming of Islam are mentioned in the same breath: "God gave you the faith of your father Abraham and named you Muslims." The collocation is certainly significant.

The Mekkan Arabs knew, and probably had known before the time of Mohammed, that according to the Hebrew records they were the descendants of Ishmael. Because of their tribal organization, with all its emphasis on family history, we should suppose them to have been pleased with the gain of a remote ancestor, even if·they felt little or no interest in his person. To Mohammed, the fact was profoundly significant. At the time when he first became aware of great religions outside Arabia, he heard of that ancient prophet Abraham, who through his second son Isaac was the founder of both the Israelite and the Christian faith, and through his elder son Ishmael was the father of the Arabian peoples. It may have been through meditation on this startling fact that he was first led to the conception of a new revelation, and a new prophet, for his own race. The Arabs were rightful heirs of the religion of Abraham; although, as he repeatedly declares, they had rejected the truth and fallen into idolatry.

It may be regarded as certain, however, that Mohammed did not believe his call to the prophetic office to be in any way the result of his own reflection on *what ought to be.* On the contrary, he was called by Allah, and the revelation for the Arabs was new, never previously given to any one. In some true sense he himself was "the first of the Muslims" (39:14). But when at length, after the Koran was well advanced, he turns to the Hebrew patriarchs, he claims them as a matter of course and speaks of them in no uncertain terms. "Abraham said, Lord, make this land [the neighborhood of Mekka] safe, and turn me and my sons away from worshipping idols. . . . . Lord, I have made some of my seed dwell in a fruitless valley, by thy holy house [the Ka'ba]. . . . . Praise to Allah, who has given me, even in my old age, Ishmael and Isaac" (14:38 ff.). "When his Lord tested Abraham with certain commands, which he obeyed, he said, I make thee an example for mankind to follow." . . . . "We laid upon Abraham and Ishmael the covenant obligation" [namely, to make the Ka'ba at Mekka a holy house, the center of the true Arabian worship; the beginning of a new stage in the religion of the world]. . . . . "And when Abraham, with Ishmael, was raising the foundations of the house, he said, Lord, accept this from us, ... make us *submissive to thee,* and make of our offspring a nation *submissive to thee,* and declare to us our ritual. . . . . Lord, send also among them a messenger of their own, who shall teach them the Book and divine wisdom" (2:118 ff.).

In the verses which immediately follow it is clearly implied that the true and final religion, Islām, was first revealed to the family of the patriarch. Vs. 126: "Abraham and Jacob gave this command to their sons: God has chosen for you the true religion; you must not die without becoming Muslims. All this plainly shows that the *submission* was originally associated in Mohammed's mind with Abraham; it was from his action, or attitude, that the religion received its name. He obeyed the commands with which Allah tested him (53:38 and 2:118).

There was one supreme test of Abraham's submission to the divine will, and it is described in an early passage in the Koran; namely, the attempted sacrifice of Ishmael (why *Ishmael*, not Isaac, has already been explained). Sura 37:100 ff.: "When the boy was old enough to share the zeal of his father, Abraham said, My son, in a vision of the night I have been shown that I am to slaughter you as a sacrifice. Say now what you think. He replied, Father, do what you are commanded; you will find me, if Allah wills, one of the steadfast. *So when they both were resigned,* and he led him to the mountain,[44] we called to him, Abraham! You have indeed fulfilled the vision; . . . . verily this was a clear test!" The verb in vs. 103, "they both *submitted*" (*aslamā*), marks the climax of the scene. Elsewhere in the Koran the verb means "embrace Islām"; here, it means simply "yield" to the will of Allah. Mohammed certainly had this supreme test in mind when he quoted the promise to the patriarch: "I make you an example for mankind to follow."

The prophet must have had the scene before his eyes, and the all-important verb in his mind, long before he produced the 37th Sura. And when he first began speaking of the "Muslims," it was the self-surrender of the two great ancestors of his people that led him to the use of the term. It required no more than ordinary foresight on the prophet's part to see, at the very outset of his public service, that a struggle was coming; and that his followers, and perhaps he himself, would be called upon to give up every precious thing, even life itself, for the sake of the cause. Submission, absolute surrender to the divine will, was a fit designation of the faith revealed to Abraham, Ishmael, and the Arabs.

---

[44] [I regard the word *jebīn* as a variation of *jebel* for the sake of the rhyme, according to the license which Mohammed allows himself in several other places in the older part of the Koran. The verb *talla* is used of "leading" a beast; see the dictionaries of Hava, Wahrmund, and Dozy].

FOURTH LECTURE

THE NARRATIVES OF THE KORAN [45]

We have seen in the preceding lectures that the Koran brings to view a rather long procession of Biblical personages, some of them mentioned several times, and a few introduced and characterized repeatedly. The experiences of the chief among them are described in stereotyped phrases, usually with bits of dramatic dialogue. The two main reasons for this parade have been indicated: first, the wish to give the new Arabian religion a clear and firm connection with the previous "religions of the Book," and especially with the Hebrew scriptures; and second, the equally important purpose which Mohammed had of showing to his countrymen how the prophets had been received in the former time; and how the religion which they preached (namely Islam) was carried on from age to age, while the successive generations of men who rejected it were punished.

In all the earliest part of the Koran there is no sustained narrative; nothing like the stories and biographies which abound in the Old Testament. The ancient heroes are hardly more than names, which the ever-turning wheel of the Koran keeps bringing before us, each one laden with the same pious exhortations.

Mohammed certainly felt this lack. He was not so unlike his countrymen as not to know the difference between the interesting and the tiresome, even if he did not feel it very strongly. We know, not only from

[45] [Weil's *Biblische Legenden der Muselmänner* (1845) contains both Koranic legends and those of later origin. Dr. Alexander Kohut gave an English translation of a number of them, with notes, in the N. Y. *Independent,* Jan. 8, 15, 22, and 29, 1891, under the title "Haggadic Elements in Arabic Legends"].

the Tradition but also from the Koran itself, that his parade of Noah, Abraham, Jonah, and their fellows was received in Mekka with jeers. His colorless scraps of history were hooted at as "old stories"; and we happen to be told how on more than one occasion he suffered from competition with a real *raconteur*. The Mekkans, like St. Paul's auditors at Athens (Acts 17:21), were ready to hear "some new thing," if only to laugh at it, but their patience was easily exhausted. One of Mohammed's neighbors, an-Naḍr ibn al-Ḥārith, took delight in tormenting the self-styled prophet, and when the latter was holding forth to a circle of hearers, he would call out, "Come over here to me, and I will give you something more interesting than Mohammed's preaching!" and then he would tell them the stories of the Persian kings and heroes; while the prophet saw his audience vanish, and was left to cherish the revenge which he took after the battle of Bedr. For the too entertaining adversary, taken captive in the battle, paid for the stories with his life.

Mohammed of course knew, even without any such bitter lesson, what his countrymen would enjoy. It is quite evident, moreover, that he himself had been greatly impressed by the tales of patriarchs, prophets, and saints which had come within his knowledge; for he was in most respects a typical Arab. And while we know, especially from the introduction to his story of Joseph, that he eventually formed the purpose of adorning his Koran with some extended narratives in order to attract as well as to convince his hearers, it probably is true that an equally strong motive was his own lively interest in these famous personages and their wonderful deeds. There are certain incidents, or bits of folk-tale, which he elaborates merely because they delight him, not at all because of any religious teaching which might be squeezed out of them. This appears, for instance, in his tales of Solomon and the Queen of Sheba, of Dhu 'l-Qarnain (Alexander the Great), and of Joseph in Egypt. His imagination played upon these things until his mind was filled with them. Here was entertainment to which the people of Mekka would listen. Even stronger, doubtless, was the hope that the Jews and Christians, who had loved these tales for many generations, would be moved by this new recognition of their divine authority, and would acknowledge Islam as a new stage in their own religious history.

It is significant that all these more pretentious attempts at story-telling fall within a brief period, the last years in Mekka and the beginning of the career in Medina. They had a purpose beyond mere instruction or mere entertainment, and when that purpose failed, there was no further attempt in the same line. As to the relative proportions of Jewish and Christian material of this nature which Mohammed had in store, it will presently appear that the supply obtained from Jewish sources greatly predominates. Moreover, in the case of the only one of the longer legends which is distinctly of Christian origin there is good evidence that it came to Mohammed through the medium of a Jewish document.

But the time when Mohammed began to put forth these few longer narratives, his Koran had grown to about one-third of the size which it ultimately attained. He must have taken satisfaction in the thought that it was beginning to have the dimensions of a sacred book, the scriptures of the new revelation in the Arabic tongue. The addition of a number of entertaining portions of history, anecdote, and biography would considerably increase its bulk, as well as its resemblance to the former sacred books.

Here appears obviously one very striking difference between the narratives of the Koran and those of the Bible. The latter were the product of consummate literary art, written at various times, for religious instruction, by men who were born story-tellers. They were preserved and handed down by a process of selection, gradually recognized as the best of their kind, and ultimately incorporated in a great anthology. In the Koran, on the contrary, we see a totally new thing—a most forbidding undertaking: the production of narrative as divine revelation, to rate from the first as inspired scripture; narrative, moreover, which had already been given permanent form in the existing sacred books. Here was a dilemma which evidently gave the Arabian prophet some trouble. If he should merely reproduce the story of Joseph, or of Jonah, wholly or in part, from the Jewish tradition, he would be charged with plagiarism. If he should tell the stories with any essential difference, he would be accused of falsifying.

A skilful narrator might have escaped this difficulty by his own literary art, producing something interesting and yet in keeping with the familiar tradition. But Mohammed was very far from being a skilful narrator. His imagination is vivid, but not creative. His characters are all alike, and they utter the same platitudes. He is fond of dramatic dialogue, but has very little sense of dramatic scene or action. The logical connection between successive episodes is often loose, sometimes wanting; and points of importance, necessary for the clear understanding of the story, are likely to be left out. There is also the inveterate habit of repetition, and a very defective sense of humor. In short, any one familiar with the style of the Koran would be likely to predict that Mohammed's tales of ancient worthies would lack most of the qualities which the typical "short story" ought to have. And the fact would be found to justify the prediction.

In Sura 11:27-51 is given a lengthy account of Noah's experiences; the building of the ark, the flood, the arrival on Mount Ararat, and God's promise for the future. It contains very little incident, but consists chiefly of the same religious harangues which are repeated scores of times throughout the Koran, uninspired and uniformly wearisome. We have the feeling that one of Noah's contemporaries who was confronted with the prospect of forty days and forty nights in the ark would prefer to take his chances with the deluge.

It must in fairness be reiterated, however, that this task of refashioning by divine afterthought would have been a problem for any narrator. Mohammed does slip out of the dilemma into which he had seemed to be forced; and the manner in which he does this is highly interesting—and instructive. The story, Jewish or Christian, is told by him in fragments; often with a repeated introductory formula that would seem to imply that the prophet had not only received his information directly from heaven, but also had been given numerous details which had not been vouchsafed to the "people of the Book." The angel of revelation brings in rather abruptly an incident or scene in the history of this or that Biblical hero with a simple introductory "And when . . . ." It says, in effect: "You remember the occasion when Moses said to his servant, I will not halt until I reach the confluence of the two rivers"; and the incident is narrated. "And then there was that time, Mohammed, when Abraham said to his people" thus and so. It is not intended, the formula implies, to tell the whole story; but more could be told, if it were necessary.

The more closely one studies the details of Mohammed's curious, and at first sight singularly ineffectual, manner of serving up these old narratives, the more clearly is gained the impression that underlying it all is the deliberate attempt to solve a problem.

The story of Joseph and his brethren is the only one in the Koran which is carried through with some semblance of completeness. It begins with the boy in the land of Canaan, and ends with the magnate in Pharaoh's kingdom, and the establishing of Jacob and his family in Egypt. It is the only instance in which an entire Sura is given up to a single subject of this nature. The following extracts will give some idea of the mode of treatment.[46]

Gabriel says to Mohammed: Remember what occurred *When Joseph said to his father, O father! I saw eleven stars and the sun and the moon prostrating themselves before me! He answered, O my boy, tell not your vision to your brothers, for they will plot against you; verily the devil is a manifest foe to mankind.* After a verse or two of religious instruction the story proceeds: *The brethren said, Surely Joseph and his brother are more beloved by our father than we; indeed he is in manifest error. Kill Joseph, or cast him away in some distant place; then we shall have our father to ourselves. One of them said, Kill not Joseph, but throw him into the bottom of the pit; then some caravan will pluck him out. They said, O father! what ails you that you will not trust us with Joseph, although we are his sincere helpers? Send him with us to-morrow to sport and play, and we will take good care of him. He said, It would grieve me that you should take him away, and I fear that the wolf will devour him*

---

[46] [On the Jewish and Mohammedan embellishment of the story of Joseph, see especially Israel Schapiro, *Die haggadischen Elemente im erzählenden Teil des Korans* (1907)].

while you are neglecting him. They said, If the wolf should devour him, while we are such a company, we should indeed be stupid! And when they went away with him and agreed to put him in the bottom of the well, we gave him this revelation: Thou shalt surely tell them of this deed of theirs when they are not aware.

They came to their father at eventide, weeping. They said, O father! we went off to run races, and left Joseph with our things, and the wolf ate him up; and you will not be believe us, though we are telling the truth. Their father of course takes the broad hint given him, that they are lying; though they bring a shirt with blood on it as evidence. He accuses them of falsehood, and reproaches them bitterly. Then is told in a very few words how the caravan came, drew Joseph out of the well, and sold him for a few dirhems to a man in Egypt.

Thereupon follows the attempt of the man's wife to entice Joseph. Any episode in which women play a part is likely to be dwelt upon by Mohammed, and he gives full space to the scenes which follow. Joseph refused at first, but was at last ready to yield, when he saw a vision which deterred him. (The nature of this is not told in the Koran, but we know from the Jewish Midrash that it was the vision of his father, with Rachel and Leah.) [47] The Koran proceeds: *They raced to the door, and she tore his shirt from behind; and at the door they met her husband. She cried, What is the penalty upon him who wished to do evil to your wife, but imprisonment or a dreadful punishment? Joseph said, She enticed me. One of her family bore witness:* [48] *If his shirt is torn in front, she tells the truth; if it is torn behind, she is lying. So when he saw that the shirt was torn from behind, he cried, This is one of your woman-tricks; verily the tricks of you women are amazing! Joseph, turn aside from this! and do you, woman, ask forgiveness for your sin.*

Then certain women of the city said, The wife of the prince tried to entice her young servant; she is utterly infatuated with him; verily we consider her in manifest error. So when she heard their treachery, she sent

---

[47] [*Sotah* 36 b; Jer. *Horayoth* 2, 46 d; *Tanhuma wayyesheb*, 9].

[48] [According to the Jewish midrash this was a baby in the cradle; *Yashar, wayyesheb* 86a–89a; see Ginzberg's note in his *Legends of the Jews*].

an invitation to them, and prepared for them a banquet,[49] *and gave each one of them a knife, and said, Come forth to them! And when they saw him, they were struck with admiration and cut their hands and cried, Good heavens! This is no human being, it is a glorious angel! Then said she, This is he concerning whom you blamed me. I did seek to entice him, but he held himself firm; and if he does not do what I command him, surely he shall be imprisoned, and be one of the ignominious. He said, Lord, the prison is my choice instead of that to which they invite me. But if thou dost not turn their wiles away from me, I shall be smitten with love for them, and shall become one of the foolish. His Lord answered his prayer, and turned their wiles away from him; verily he is one who hears and knows.*

This is characteristic of the angel Gabriel's manner of spoiling a good story. Aside from the fact that we are left in some uncertainty as to Joseph's firmness of character, it is not evident what the episode of the banquet had to do with the course of events; nor why the ladies were provided with knives; nor why Joseph, after all, was put in prison. These things are all made plain in the Midrash, however.[50]

The account of Joseph's two companions in the prison, and of his ultimate release, is given in very summary fashion. *There entered the prison with him two young men. One of them said, I see myself pressing out wine; and the other said, I see myself carrying bread upon my head, and the birds eating from it. Tell us the interpretation of this.* After a religious discourse of some length, Joseph gives them the interpretation; and it is implied, though not definitely said, that his prediction was completely fulfilled. The dream of Pharaoh is then introduced abruptly. *The king said, Verily I see seven fat cows which seven lean ones are devouring; and seven green ears of grain and others which are dry. O you princes, explain to me my vision, if you can interpret a vision.* The princes naturally give it up. The king's butler remembers Joseph, though several years have elapsed, and he is summoned from the prison. He refuses to

---

[49] [*Yashar, l.c.,* 87a–87b; *Tanhuma wayyesheb,* 5. The former may have used the Koran (Ginzberg)].

[50] [*Yalkut* I, 146; *Midrash Hag-Gadol* (ed. Schechter), I, 590].

come out, however, until his question has been answered: "What was in the mind of those women who cut their hands? Verily my master knows their wiles." The women are questioned, and both the officer's wife and her companions attest Joseph's innocence. He is then brought out, demands to be set over the treasuries of all Egypt, and the king complies.

Joseph's brethren now enter the story again. Nothing is said about a famine in the land of Canaan, nor is any other reason given for their arrival, they simply appear. The remainder of the tale is in the main a straightforward, somewhat fanciful, condensation of the version given in the book of Genesis, with some lively dialogue. There are one or two touches from the Midrash. Jacob warns his sons not to enter the city by a single gate. The Midrash gives the reason; [51] the Koran leaves the Muslim commentators to guess—as of course they easily can. When the cup is found in Benjamin's sack, and he is proclaimed a thief, his brethren say, "If he has stolen, a brother of his stole before him." The commentators are at their wits' end to explain how Joseph could have been accused of stealing. The explanation is furnished by the Midrash, which remarks at this point that Benjamin's *mother* before him had stolen; [52] referring of course to the time when Rachel carried off her father's household gods (Gen. 31:19–35).

The occasion when Joseph makes himself known to his brethren is not an affecting scene in the Koran, as it is in the Hebrew story. The narrator's instinct which would cause him to work up to a climax was wanting in the Mekkan prophet's equipment. The brethren come to Egypt for the third time, appear before Joseph, and beg him to give them good measure. He replies, *Do you know what you did to Joseph and his brother, in the time of your ignorance? They said, Are you then Joseph? He answered, I am Joseph, and this is my brother. God has been gracious to us. Whoever is pious and patient,—God will not suffer the righteous to lose their reward.* This is simple routine; no one in the party appears to be excited.

[51] [*Ber. Rab.* 91, 6; *Tan.* B, I, 193 f., 195; *Midrash Hag-Gadol* I, 635].
[52] [*Ber. Rab.* 102, 8; *Tan.* B, I, 198; MHG I, 653].

Jacob wept for Joseph until the constant flow of tears destroyed his eye-sight. Joseph therefore, when the caravan bringing his parents to Egypt set out from Canaan, sent his shirt by a messenger, saying that it would restore his father's sight. Jacob recognizes the odor of the shirt while yet a long distance from it, and says, "Verily I perceive the smell of Joseph!" The messenger arrives, throws the shirt on Jacob's face, and the sight is restored. The story ends with the triumphant entrance into Egypt, and the fulfilment of the dream of Joseph's boyhood; they have all bowed down to him.

Before the impressive homily which closes the chapter, Gabriel says to Mohammed (verse 103): "This tale is one of the secrets which we reveal to you"; and he adds, referring to Joseph's brethren: "You were not with them when they agreed upon their plan and were treacherous." [53] This might seem to be a superfluous reminder; but its probable intent is to say here with especial emphasis, not only to Mohammed but also to others, that no inspired prophet, Arabian or Hebrew, can narrate details, or record dialogues, other than those which have been revealed to him. Conversely, every prophet has a right to his own story.

The tale of Solomon and the Queen of Sheba (27:16–45) gives further illustration of Mohammed's manner of retelling in leaps and bounds. Here also is shown, even more clearly than in the story of Joseph, his tendency to be mysterious. The material of the narrative is taken from the Jewish haggada,[54] but much is omitted that is quite necessary for the understanding of the story. Change of scene is not indicated, and the progress of events is often buried under little homilies delivered by the principal characters (I omit the homilies).

Solomon was David's heir; and he said: O you people! We have been taught the speech of birds, and we have been given everything. Verily this is a manifest favor.

There were assembled for Solomon his hosts of jinn, and men, and

<hr>

[53] [Observe also the use of this formula in 3:39 and 28:44, 46].
[54] [I omit the references, which are given by Geiger, pp. 181–186].

birds; and they proceeded together until they came to the Valley of the Ants.[55] *An ant cried out: O you ants! Get into your dwellings, lest Solomon and his armies crush you without knowing it. Solomon smiled, laughing at her speech, and said: O Lord, arouse me to thankfulness for thy favor. . . .* Here follows a homily. We are left in some doubt as to whether the ants suffered any damage; for the tale proceeds:

He reviewed the birds, and said, How is it that I do not see the hoopoe? Is he among the absent? I surely will torture him with severe tortures, or I will slaughter him, or else he shall bring me an authoritative excuse. He was not long absent, however; and he said: I have learned something which you knew not. I bring you from Sheba sure information. I found a woman ruling over them; she has been given all things, and she has a mighty throne. I found her and her people worshipping the sun. Solomon said, We shall see whether you have told the truth, or are one of the liars. Take this letter of mine, and throw it before them. Then return, and we will see what reply they make.

She said: O you chieftains! A noble letter has been thrown before me. It is from Solomon, and it says, "In the name of God, the merciful Rahmān; Do not resist me, but come to me resigned." O you chieftains! Advise me in this matter. They said, We are mighty men of valor, but it is for you to command. She said, When kings enter a city, they plunder it, and humble its mighty men. I will send them a present, and see what my messenger brings back.

Solomon preaches to the messenger, threatens him and his people, and bids him return. Then he addresses his curious army: Which of you will bring me her throne, before they come in submission? (There was need of haste, for after the queen had once accepted Islam, Solomon would have no right to touch her property.) *A demon of the jinn said, I will bring it, before you can rise from your seat. He who had the knowledge of the Book said, I will bring it before your glance can turn. So when he saw the throne set down before him, he said, This is of the favor of my Lord* (and he adds some improving reflections of a general nature). The native

[55] [This episode is probably Mohammed's own creation, based on his hearing of Prov. 6:6–8].

commentators explain that the throne was brought to Solomon under ground, the demons digging away the earth in front and filling it in behind; and all in the twinkling of an eye—according to the promise. The reader must not suppose, however, that this underground transit was from South Arabia to Palestine. Mohammed left out the part of the story which tells how Solomon's army was transported through the air to a place in the neighborhood of the queen's capital.

He said, Disguise her throne! We shall see whether she is rightly guided, or not. So when she came, it was said, Was your throne like this? She replied, It might be the same. Then they said to her, Enter the court! And when she saw it, she supposed it to be a pool of water, and uncovered her legs to wade through. But Solomon (who was not absent) *said: It is a court paved with glass! She said, O Lord, verily I have been wrong; but I am now resigned, with Solomon, to Allah the Lord of the Worlds!* That is, she became a Muslim. The Koran drops the story here, not concerned to tell that Solomon married her.

Of the queen's interest in the *wisdom* of Solomon, which plays such a part in the Biblical narrative, and still more in the Jewish midrash, not a word is said here. This feature must have been known to Mohammed, but it did not suit his purpose. His own quaintly disjointed sketch doubtless achieved the effect which he intended. The mystery of the half-told would certainly impress the Mekkans; and the Jews would say, *We know* these incidents, and there is much more of the story in our books! So Mohammed would achieve a double triumph.

The account of Jonah and his experiences given in 37:139-148 is unique in the Koran. The whole Biblical narrative, without any external features, is told in a single breath, a noteworthy example of condensation. Even the hymn of prayer and praise from the belly of the whale receives mention in vs. 143. As has already been observed, Jonah is the only one of all the fifteen *Nebiim Acharonim* to receive mention in the Koran. The name of the Hebrew prophet is given (here as elsewhere) in a form ultimately based on the Greek; seeming to indicate—as in so many other cases—an origin outside Arabia. The nutshell summary may have been made by

Mohammed himself, after hearing the story read or repeated (though he nowhere else condenses in this headlong but complete fashion); or it may have been dictated to him, and then by him decorated, clause by clause, with his rhymed verse-endings.

Verily, Jonah was one of the missionaries. When he fled to the laden ship, he cast lots, and was of those who lost. The whale swallowed him, for he was blameworthy; and had it not been that he celebrated God's praises, he surely would have remained in its belly until the day when men rise from the dead. So we cast him upon the barren shore; and he was sick; and we made a gourd to grow over him. And we sent him to a hundred thousand, or more; and they believed, and we gave them prosperity for a time.

The narrative of "Saul and Goliath" (Ṭālūt and Jālūt) gives a good illustration of the way in which the Mekkan prophet's memory sometimes failed him.

The leaders of the children of Israel ask their prophet to give them a king (2:247). He argues with them, but eventually says: *God has appointed Ṭālūt as your king. They said, How shall he be king over us, when we are more worthy to rule than he, and he has no abundance of wealth? He answered, God has chosen him over you, and has made him superior in knowledge and in stature* (cf. 1 Sam. 9:2). . . . . *So when Ṭālūt went forth with the armies, he said: God will test you by a river: Whoever drinks of it is not of mine; those who do not taste of it, or who only sip it from the hand, are my army. So all but a few drank of it. When they had passed beyond it, some said, We are powerless this day against Jālūt and his forces. But those who believed that they must meet God said, How often has a little band conquered a numerous army, by the will of God! He is with those who are steadfast. So they went forth against the army, ... and by the will of God they routed them; and David slew Jālūt, and God gave him the kingdom.*

Here, obviously, is confusion with the tale of Gideon and his three hundred picked men (Judg. 7:4–7). The casual way in which David finally enters the narrative is also noteworthy.

The first half of the 28th Sura (vss. 2–46) gives an interesting outline of the early history of Moses, following closely the first four chapters of Exodus. It illustrates both the general trustworthiness of Mohammed's memory, for it includes practically every item contained in these chapters, often with reproduction of the very words; and also, a certain freedom in his treatment of the Hebrew material, for he introduces, for his own convenience, some characteristic little changes and embellishments. This is the longest continuous extract from The Old Testament which the Koran contains. Mohammed does not treat the story as an episode in Hebrew history, but carries it through, in his cryptic fashion, without any specific mention of the "children of Israel." The Sura dealing with Joseph and his brethren had already been put forth (it can hardly be doubted), but he makes no allusion to it, nor to the entrance of Hebrews into Egypt.

Pharaoh exalted himself in the earth, and divided his people into parties. One portion of them he humbled, slaughtering their male children, and suffering their females to live; verily he was of those who deal wickedly. But we were purposing to show favor to those who were humbled in the land, and to make them leaders and heirs; to establish them in the earth, and to show Pharaoh and Haman and their hosts what they had to fear from them.

Haman appears consistently in the Koranic narrative (also in Suras 29 and 40) as Pharaoh's vizier. Rabbinic legends mention several advisers of Pharaoh (Geiger, 153), but Mohammed had in mind a more important officer. He had heard the story of Esther (and of course retained it in memory), and both name and character of the arch anti-Semite appealed strongly to his imagination. That he transferred the person, as well as the name, to Egypt is not at all likely. Gabriel knew that there were two Hamans.

And we gave this revelation to Moses' mother: Give him suck; and when you fear for his life, put him into the river; and be not fearful, nor grieved; for we will restore him to you, and make him one of our apostles. So Pharaoh's family plucked him out, to be an enemy and a misfortune to them; verily Pharaoh and Haman and their hosts were sinners. Pharaoh's wife said, Here is joy for me and thee! Slay him not; haply he may be of use to us, or we may adopt him as a son (repeating the words which Potiphar uttered to his wife, in the case of Joseph). *But they knew not what was impending.*

Events develop as in the Biblical narrative. Moses' mother is hindered by divine intervention from letting out the secret, in her anxiety. The child's sister follows him, keeping watch, unobserved, from a distance. The babe refuses the breast of Egyptian nurses, as the Talmud declares (*Sotah,* 12 b); so it comes about that he is restored to his mother. Arrived at manhood, Moses enters "the city" stealthily, and finds two men fighting: "The one, a member of his party; the other, of his enemies." He is called upon for help, and kills the "enemy" with his fist—the blow of an expert boxer. He repents of his deed, utters a prayer, and is forgiven; but on the following day, as he enters the city cautiously and in apprehension, the same scene is set: the same man is fighting with another of the hostile party, and cries out for help. Moses reproaches his comrade ("Verily you are a manifest scoundrel!"), but again intervenes. As he approaches, to deal another knock-out blow, the intended victim cries out: "O Moses, do you mean to kill me, as you killed a man yesterday? You are only aiming to be a tyrant in the land, not to be one of the virtuous!" Just then a man came running from the other end of the city, saying, "O Moses, the nobles are taking counsel to kill you! So be off; I am giving you good advice." Thereupon Moses starts for Midian.

The account of the happenings in Midian is given with characteristic improvement. Here again is illustrated the prophet's lively interest in those scenes in which women figure prominently. He doubles the romance in the story, patterning it, in a general way, upon the account of Jacob and Rachel. *Seven* daughters at the well are too many, he recognizes only *two;* and Moses serves them gallantly, thereafter accompanying them home. *One of them came to him, walking bashfully, and said: My father is calling for you, to pay you for drawing water for us. And when he came to him, and told him his story, he said, Fear not; you have escaped from an impious people.* Mohammed neither names the father of the girls nor shows the least interest in him; he is merely a necessary property of the story. We could wish, however, that Mohammed (or Moses) had shown a more decided preference for the one or the other of the daughters. *One of them said, O father, hire him! The best that you hire are the strong and trusty. He said: I wish to marry you to one of these two daughters of mine, on the condition that you work for me eight years;* [56] *and if you shall wish to make it a full ten years, that rests with you. I do not wish to be hard on you, and you will find me, if God wills, one of the upright. Moses replied: So be it between thee and me; whichever of the two terms I fulfil, there will be no grudge against me; and God is the witness of what we say. So when Moses had completed the term* [which term?], *and journeyed away with his family* [which daughter?], *he became aware of a fire on the side of the mountain. He said to his family, Wait here; I have discovered a fire. Perhaps I may bring you news from it, or a firebrand, so that you may warm yourselves. So when he came up to it, a voice called to him out of the tree, on the right side of the wady in the sacred valley, O Moses! I am God, the Lord of the Worlds. Throw down your rod. And when he saw it move as though it were a serpent, he fled from it without turning back. O Moses, draw nigh and fear not, for you are safe!*

The narrative then recounts the miracle of the leprous hand, the appointment of Aaron, and the first unsuccessful appearance before Pharaoh and his magicians. Instead of the story of the brickmaking task, which occupies the fifth chapter of Exodus, Mohammed introduces a feature which he adapts from the story of the Tower of Babel. *Pharaoh said: O you nobles! I know not that you have any god except myself. So now, Haman, burn for me bricks of clay, and build me a tower, so that I may mount up to the god of Moses; verily I consider him a liar. And he and his hosts behaved arrogantly and unjustly in the earth, nor considered that they shall be brought back to us. So we took him and his armies and cast them into the sea; behold therefore how the wicked are punished.*

Gabriel concludes by saying to the prophet (as at the end of the story

---

[56] [Mohammed of course avoids the number given in the Biblical story of Jacob].

of Joseph): *You were not on the west side when we decreed the matter for Moses, nor were you a witness; . . . . nor were you dwelling among the people of Midian. . . . . It is only by mercy from your Lord (that these things are revealed to you).*

This narrative of the early life of Moses is particularly instructive, not only as illustrating Mohammed's manner of retelling the Biblical stories, but also as showing, better than any other part of the Koran, the freedom with which he could adorn his own account with properties deliberately taken over by him from other Biblical stories with which he was familiar. That he felt himself to be quite within his rights, *as a prophet,* in so doing, may be considered certain.

The 18th Sura holds a peculiar place in the Koran. The narratives of which it is mainly composed are at once seen to be different in character from the types which elsewhere are so familiar. While in every other part of the sacred book Mohammed draws either upon the Biblical and rabbinic material or else upon Arabian lore, in Sura 18 we are given a sheaf of legends from the world-literature. The stories have the characteristic Mohammedan flavor, it is true; yet the Sura has distinctly an atmosphere of its own, and the prophet makes no allusion elsewhere to any part of its narrative material.

First comes the famous legend of the Seven Sleepers of Ephesus. Certain youths fled to a cave in the mountains to escape the persecution of the Christians under Decius (c. 250 A.D.). Their pursuers found their hiding place, and walled it up. They were miraculously preserved in a Rip van Winkle sleep, and came forth some two hundred years later, in the reign of the emperor Theodosius II, when some workmen happened to take away the stones. The legend arose before the end of the fifth century, and soon made its way all over western Asia and Europe. Since it is a Christian tale, and since also there is particular mention of the Christians in the opening verses of the Sura, some have drawn the conclusion that this little collection of stories was designed by the prophet to attract the adherents of that faith especially. There is, however, nothing else in the

chapter to give support to this theory, while on the other hand there
is considerable evidence that even the opening legend came to Mohammed
through the medium of a Jewish document. Aside from the fact that
Muslim tradition represents the Jews of Mekka as interested in this
tale (see Beiḍāwī on vs. 23), and the additional fact that each of the
following narratives in the Sura appears to be derived from a Jewish
recension, there is a bit of internal evidence here which should not be
overlooked. In vs. 18 the speaker says, "Send some one . . . . to the city,
and *let him find out where the cleanest food is to be had,* and bring
provision from it." This emphasized care as to the legal fitness of the
food at once suggests a Jewish version of the legend. A Christian
narrator, if the idea occurred to him at all, would have need to specify
what he meant (e. g. food offered to idols). It is to be observed that
this motive does not occur in the homily of Jacob of Sarug, nor is there
anything corresponding to it in any of the early Christian versions which
I have seen; those for instance published by Guidi, *I Sette Dormienti,*
and Huber, *Die Wanderlegende.* There is no Christian element in the
story, as it lies before us in the Koran; it might well be an account of the
persecution of Israelite youths.

As usual, the narrative begins without scene or setting. Gabriel says
to Mohammed, *Do you not think, then, that the heroes of the story of
the Cave and of ar-Raqīm* [57] *were of our marvellous signs? When the
youths took refuge in the cave, they said, Lord, show us thy mercy, and
guide us aright in this affair of ours. So we sealed up their hearing in
the cave for a number of years. Then at length we awakened them; and
we would see which of the two parties made better calculation of the
time which had elapsed. . . . . You could see the sun, when it arose, pass
to the right of their cave, and when it set, go by them on the left; while
they were in a chamber within. . . . . You would have thought them
awake, but they were asleep; and we turned them over, now to the right,
now to the left; and their dog stretched out his paws at the entrance.*

[57] [This curious name, as has already been said (see p. 46), is the result of an easy misreading of the name *Decius* written in the Aramaic script].

If you had come upon them suddenly, you would have fled from them in fear. Then we awakened them, to let them question one another. One said, How long have you tarried? Some answered, A day, or part of a day. Others said, Your Lord knows best how long; but send one, with this money, into the city; let him find where the cleanest food is to be had, and bring back provision; let him be courteous, and not make you known to any one. If they get knowledge of you, they will stone you, or bring you back to their religion; then you will fare ill forever. So we made their story known; . . . . and the people of the city disputed about them. Some said, Build a structure over them; their Lord knows best about them. Those whose opinion won the day said, We will build over them a house of worship.

The verses which follow show that the prophet was heckled about this tale, and felt that he had been incautious. The existing versions of the legend differed, or were non-committal, as to the number of the Sleepers. Some of Mohammed's hearers were familiar with the story, and now asked him for exact information. It may be useless to conjecture who these hearers were, but the probability certainly inclines toward the Jews, who heckled Mohammed on other occasions, and of all the inhabitants of Mekka were those most likely to be acquainted with this literature. If, as otherwise seems probable, it came to the prophet's knowledge through them, and in an anthology made for their use, they would very naturally be disposed to make trouble for him when he served out the legends as a part of his divine revelation. The Koran proceeds:

They will say, three, and the fourth was their dog; or they will say, five, and the sixth was their dog (guessing at the secret); others will say, seven, and their dog made eight. Say: My Lord best knows their number, and there are few others who know. Do not dispute with them, unless as to what is certain; nor apply to any one of them for information. Say not in regard to a thing, I will do it tomorrow; but say, If God wills. Remember your Lord, when you have forgotten, and say, Mayhap my Lord will guide me, that I may draw near to the truth in this matter. They remained in their cave three hundred years, and nine more. Say: God knows best how long they stayed.

After this comes (vss. 31–42) a parable of a familiar sort: the god-fearing poor man, and his arrogant neighbor the impious rich man, upon whom punishment soon descends. This might be Jewish, or Christian, or (much less probably) native Arabic. It is not difficult to believe that Mohammed himself could have composed it entire, but more likely it is abbreviated by him from something which formed part of the (Aramaic?) anthology which was his main source in this Sura.

Farther on (verse 59) begins the story of Moses and his attendant, journeying in search of the fountain of life. This is a well known episode in the legend of Alexander the Great, whose place is here taken by Moses. Mohammed certainly was not the author of the substitution, but received it with the rest of the story. To all appearance, we have here a Jewish popular adaptation of the legend. The opening words of the Koranic version, however, take us far back of Alexander the Great. Moses says to his attendant, "I will not halt until I reach the meeting-place of the two rivers, though I go on for many years!" Now this brings in a bit of very ancient mythology. In the old Babylonian epic of Gilgamesh the hero, after many labors and trials, goes forth in search of immortality. He hears of a favorite of the gods, Utnapishtim, who has been granted eternal life. After great exertions Gilgamesh arrives at the place where this ancient hero dwells, *at the confluence of the streams.* Utnapishtim attempts to give some help, but Gilgamesh fails of his main purpose. The Koran proceeds:

Now when they reached the confluence, they forgot their fish, and it made its way into the river in quick passage. After they had proceeded farther, Moses said to his attendant, Bring out our luncheon, for we have suffered weariness in this journey of ours. He answered: Do you see, when we halted at the rock I forgot the fish (and only Satan made me forget to mention the fact), and it took its way into the river marvellously. He cried, That is the place which we were seeking! And they turned about straightway on their track. They had taken with them a dried fish for food, and the magical water restored it to life. This motive occurs in other legends; but the ultimate source of the main account here is plainly the narrative in Pseudo-Callisthenes, which in the forms known to us contains also this particular incident. Gilgamesh, Alexander, and Moses all find the place of which they were in search, but Moses' fish alone achieves immortality. It is important to observe, moreover, that Moses, like Gilgamesh, finds the ancient hero to whom God had granted eternal life. The Koran does not name him, but he is well known to Muslim legend by the name al-Khiḍr ("Evergreen"?).[58]

The story of Moses now enters a new phase. He becomes temporarily the peripatetic pupil of the immortal saint; the attendant who figured in the preceding narrative disappears from sight. *So they found a Servant of ours, to whom we had granted mercy, and whom we had taught our wisdom. Moses said to him, May I follow you, with the understanding that you will impart to me of your wisdom? He replied, You will not be able to bear with me. For how can you restrain yourself in regard to matters which your knowledge does not compass? He said, You will find me patient (if God wills), and I will not oppose you in anything. If then you will follow me, he said, you must not question me about any matter, until I give you account of it.*

The wise man who does strange things, ultimately explained by him, is well known to folk-lore. The amazement, or distress, of the onlooker is of course always an essential feature. The penalty of inquisitiveness, "If you question, we must part!" (as in the tale of Lohengrin), might naturally occur to any narrator—especially when the wise man is an immortal, who of necessity must soon disappear from mortal eyes. This feature, however, is not at all likely to have been Mohammed's own invention, but on the contrary is an essential part of the story which he repeats. Whoever the inquisitive mortal may have been in the legend's first estate, as it came to the Arabian prophet it was a Jewish tale told of Moses. More than this cannot be said at present.

The Servant of God scuttles a boat which he and Moses had borrowed; kills a youth whom they happen to meet; and takes the trouble to rebuild a tottering wall in a city whose inhabitants had refused them

---

[58] [For the literature dealing with these ancient folk-tales and their use in the Koran, see the notes in Nöldeke-Schwally, 140 ff., and Horovitz, *Koranische Untersuchungen,* 141 ff. See also what was said, in regard to the probable form in which these legends were available at Mekka, in the Second Lecture, p. 36].

shelter. On each of the three occasions Moses expresses his concern at the
deed. Twice he is pardoned, but on his third failure to restrain himself
the Servant dismisses him, after giving him information which showed
each of the three deeds to have been fully justified.

Last of all, in this Sura, comes the narrative of the "Two-Horned"
hero—again Alexander the Great. Verse 82 introduces the account with
the words: "They will ask you about Dhu l'-Qarnain ('him of the two
horns')". What interrogators did Gabriel have in mind? According to
the Muslim tradition, the Jews were intended; and this is for every reason
probable. The Koranic story, like its predecessor which told of the
fountain of life, is based on Pseudo-Callisthenes; but it contains traits
which point to a Jewish adaptation. Haggada and midrash had dealt
extensively with Alexander; and (as in the case of the story of the Seven
Sleepers) no other of the prophet's hearers would have been so likely
to test his knowledge of great events and personages. What Mohammed
had learned about Alexander seems in fact to have been very little. He
tells how the hero journeyed, first to the setting of the sun, and then to
the place of its rising; appearing in either place as an emissary of the
One God. The major amount of space, however, is given to the account
of the protection against Gog and Magog (Yājūj and Mājūj), the great
wall built by Alexander. This fantasy on traits of Hebrew mythology
suggests the haggada, and increases the probability, already established,
that all of the varied folk-lore in this 18th Sura was derived from a
Jewish collection of stories and parables (probably a single document)
designed for popular instruction and entertainment.

When to the longer narratives which have been described are added
the many brief bits mentioned in the preceding lecture, and the fact is
borne in mind that Mohammed's purpose is to give only a selection, or
occasionally mere fragments, it is evident that he had imbibed a great
amount of material of this nature. It included (1) Biblical narrative more
or less altered; (2) Jewish haggada, in already fixed form; (3) a small
amount of material of ultimately Christian origin; and (4) legends be-

longing to the world-literature, available at Mekka in the Aramaic language. The treatment is Mohammed's own, with abridgment in his characteristic manner, and embellishment mainly homiletic. For the chronological and other blunders he alone is responsible. Finally, it is to be borne in mind that the prophet knew, better than we know, what he was trying to do. In the case of some habitual traits which we find amusing, such as the grasshopper-like mode of progressing, and the omission of essential features, we may well question to what extent they show shrewd calculation rather than childlike inconsequence. Since his purpose was not to reproduce the Jewish scriptures, but to give the Arabs a share in them, his method may be judged by the result. His hearers were not troubled by the violation of literary canons, for they felt themselves in the presence of a divine message intended for them especially. If they were mystified, they were also profoundly stirred and stimulated. Around all these Koranic narratives there is, and was from the first, the atmosphere of an Arabian revelation, and they form a very characteristic and important part of the prophet's great achievement.

MOHAMMED'S LEGISLATION

While Mohammed was in Mekka, before the flight to Yathrib, he was not in a position to put forth laws. He and his comparatively few adherents were barely tolerated by their fellow-citizens, and their conduct was closely watched. It was made clear to them that while they remained in Mekka they must do as the Mekkans did. Mohammed himself, during all this time, can hardly have meditated any formal and definite prescription for his "Muslims" beyond faith in God and his prophet, simple rites of prayer, and the universally recognized duties of kinship, charity, and fair dealing. Even after the emigration, during the first year or thereabouts, while the Muhājirūn ("emigrants") and the Anṣār ("helpers" in Yathrib) and the prophet himself were getting their bearings, the time for formal legislation had not come.

There was another important consideration which postponed the necessity. It was not yet clear to Mohammed how he was to be received by the Jews and Christians, especially the former, now that he was established, with a greatly increased following, beyond the reach of persecution. The Jews had their laws and customs, which already were fairly well known to him. If he should be accepted by them as the Arabian Prophet, continuing the line of their own prophets and, as he repeatedly insists, "confirming what they had already received," then the Jewish regulations, in some considerable part, might be normative for the Muslims. He instructed his followers to pray with their faces toward Jerusalem, and to abstain from certain foods which were prohibited in the Mosaic code. It was of course obvious to him that not all the Jewish dietary laws and

religious observances could be prescribed for the Arabs; and aside from
this he wished, as we have seen (p. 69), to retain every native rite and
custom compatible with strict monotheism and civilized usage. The
possibility of some compromise, or mutual agreement, would have to be
considered.

It is noteworthy that Mohammed's idea of the "people of the Book,"
as regards their influence in Arabia and their importance to his cause,
does not appear to have been changed by his removal from the one city
to the other; also, that the attitude of his Jewish hearers, as a whole,
toward his teaching (so far as can be shown by the allusions and addresses
to them in the Koran) was substantially the same during his last years
in Mekka as it was in Medina at the outset of his career in that city. The
Jewish population of the Hijaz was both extensive and homogeneous, and
the settlement at Mekka was by no means small. There was constant
communication from city to city, and the Israelite estimate of the Arabian
prophet was well understood and the same all the way from Mekka and
Ṭā'if to Teima. Mohammed nevertheless had received considerable encouragement from certain Jews in Mekka. Some had accepted Islam;
others, doubtless, had flattered him, or even hailed him as a prophet,
in the hope of bringing him over to Judaism. He certainly exaggerates
this Jewish support in such Mekkan passages as 13:36 ("Those to whom
we gave the scriptures rejoice in that which has been revealed to thee");
28:52 f.; 29:46; 46:9, etc. Other contemporary passages show that he had
considerable controversy with the "men of the scriptures," though he
tried to avoid it, and hoped that these stubborn opponents would soon
see the light. Thus for example 6:20, 89, 148; 7:168; 28:48. "Contend
with the people of the Book only in a mild way—except with those who
are a bad lot" (29:45).[59] It is plain that he was desperately desirous of
obtaining from the Jews some general and authoritative recognition, not

---

[59] [I. e. the professed enemies who are merely trying to make trouble; the same phrase
in 2:145. There is no sufficient reason for supposing that the clause here quoted refers to
the hostile activity of the Jews in Medina, and thus permits taking up arms against them
(Nöldeke-Schwally, 155). Mohammed and his adherents had encountered plenty of dis-
agreeable hostility while he was in Mekka, and even Gabriel would not require the Muslims
to answer boorish insults politely].

merely the adherence of a few. The Jews of Mekka, for their part, had no reason to offer formal opposition to a small and persecuted sect. The strife between the adherents of the new revelation and the unbelievers of Qoreish may even have been entertaining to them. Mohammed very naturally persuaded himself that their prevailing indifference meant more than mere tolerance, and that the support which he had received from a minority would eventually be given by the majority.

The change came with the removal to Yathrib. It was not so much a change in the attitude of the Jews as in Mohammed's comprehension of the attitude. A new political situation had suddenly arisen. The Muslims were in possession of the city, yet even now were a small force in the Hijaz, and sure to have trouble soon. The Jewish settlements in the outskirts of the city were large, wealthy, and in part well fortified. It was no time for long parleying. Mohammed was lord of the city (henceforth "Medina"; *madīnat an-Nabī*, "the city of the Prophet"), and in a position to demand—as he certainly did—that the "people of the Book" should now at last join the evidently triumphing cause, acknowledge the authority of its leader, and profess faith in the new Arabian scriptures which "confirmed" their own. Neutrality would be a great danger—as it proved to be. For the first time since Mohammed's first appearance as the Arabian prophet, a large and representative body of the Jews was compelled to "show its hand." It did so, and the reply was negative; they would not accept him as a prophet continuing their line, nor his book as in any way on a par with their own.

Mohammed could not accept this answer as final while there remained any possibility of gaining the support which had seemed to him indispensable. It is quite evident in the long and desperate argument which occupies a large part of the second Sura that he had not abandoned all hope. Some Jews in Medina, as in Mekka, came over to his side, while still others showed themselves undecided (2:70 f.). He continues to speak of their unbelievers as "a party" (2:95, 115, 141); and so also in some of the following Suras. He repeatedly reminds the children of Israel (e. g. in 2:44) that they had been preferred by God above all other human beings. There is also the remarkable utterance in 2:59: "Verily the Muslims, the Jews, the Christians, the Ṣābi'ans, those who believe in God, and the last day, and who do what is right; they shall have their reward with their Lord; there shall come no fear upon them, nor shall they be grieved." The verse is repeated in 5:73; but Mohammed could not long continue to admit all that this seemed to declare, and presently (in 3:79) we read: "Whoever follows any other religion than Islam, it will not be accepted from him, and in the world to come he will be among the lost."

The time came, not long after the Hijra, when it was clear to the prophet that he must stand on his own feet, with Islam definitely against all other religions, and bound to triumph over them by force—as the famous coin-inscription, derived from the Koran, declares (9:33; 61:9). His failure to gain the support of the Jews was the most bitter disappointment of his career.[60] It became increasingly evident to him that he had nothing to expect from them but opposition. They now held a peculiar position in relation to the Muslim community. Mohammed was soon at war with the Mekkans, and in constant danger of trouble with the Bedouin Arabs, who merely wished to help the stronger side, for their own benefit. The Jews for a time held the balance of power. They were perfectly willing to see Mohammed's party wiped out by the Mekkan armies. They had no intention of taking up arms, but did not hesitate to stir up disaffection in the city, and to give secret aid to the enemy. Mohammed, for his part, was soon more than ready to come to open conflict with them, and in the end dealt with them ruthlessly.

The prophet cut loose from the Jews of Arabia, but by no means from Judaism. It was not merely that his Islam was still, and for all time, the faith of the Hebrew prophets; he was now the supreme ruler of a religious and social order which unquestionably must follow the pattern which God, through his prophets, had prescribed. Ever since the day when the conception of holy scripture, of a progressive divine revelation, and of the great line of prophets which he was to continue had dawned upon him, he had been eagerly interested in the laws and customs of the "people of the Book," and had done his best to become familiar with them. His Jewish teachers had taught him, and he could see for himself

[60] Ahrens, "Christliches im Qoran" (ZDMG. IX), 155 ff., seems hardly to appreciate this].

the vast superiority of their rules of life over the practices of pagan Arabia. Whether the Jews of Mekka and Medina were worthy of their inheritance, or not, the statutes of Moses and the oral legislation were the word of God and never to be set aside. They were indeed to be modified, by divine prescription, as will presently appear. Now that the Arabian prophet found himself called upon to legislate for his community, without the consultation which he probably had counted upon, he could only take his pattern from the one divinely ordered community of which he had first-hand knowledge.

We should expect to find in the Koran, at this juncture, that Mohammed turned his face toward the Christians, emphasizing their share in the great revelation, and perhaps also adopting some characteristic part of their ritual. We do in fact seem to find that he did both of these things. Soon after arriving at Medina he instituted the fast of Ramaḍān (2:181 ff.), very probably patterned on the Lenten fast of the Christians. In the third year of the Hijra, in the Sura entitled "The Family of Imrān," he devoted verses 30–59 to the Christians; and soon thereafter, in Sura 4, verses 155–157 and 169 f. The fifth Sura, entitled "The Table," i. e. the table of the Eucharist (112 ff.), gives a large amount of space to the Christians and their beliefs; always exalting Jesus the Prophet, but controverting the tenets of his followers. It is abundantly evident, here as elsewhere, that he knew very little about the Christians, and hardly anything in regard to their scriptures. Whatever authority they possessed was essentially that of the Hebrew legislation; and it was here, of necessity, that Mohammed sought and found his own guidance.

The need was not merely, nor chiefly, of prescriptions relating to the Muslim ritual; there was urgent and rapidly increasing demand for regulation of business transactions and other social relations. The Arabian scriptures were only begun. Mohammed's followers could not sit down and enjoy their new religion, for as yet they hardly knew what it was; they were full of questions and objections, brought forth by new circumstances. "Allah and his prophet" must be coördinated with the most important current events, and the practical problems which were constantly arising must have an authoritative solution. The Muslims must

be told in the Koran why they defeated the Mekkans at Bedr, and why
they themselves were defeated at Ohod; but also, what was prescribed
for them in regard to blood revenge and retaliation, and how the spoils
of war were to be divided. Laws regulating the Muslim family, such as
those in the opening portion of the fourth Sura, were very soon demanded; and more than one Sura was required in order to shed a
divine light on the most serious of the prophet's own domestic difficulties.

Both the amount and the quality of Mohammed's legislation in the
Koran, especially in the regulation of the worldly affairs of public and
private life, are remarkable. The laws bear eloquent testimony to his
energy, his sincerity (often somewhat childlike), and his great fund of
practical wisdom. An especially important feature is the very obvious
relation which many of these enactments bear to the Biblical and rabbinical prescriptions. The extent to which the Koran is dependent on
these earlier sources has not often been realized. The order is now not
"the law and the prophets," but "the prophets and the law"; and in both
great divisions the basis is as firm as an Arabian prophet could make it.
When all has been said, however, the originality of the man remains
more impressive than his dependence.

In one highly important passage (7:156) Mohammed plainly declares
his own legislation to be a revision and improvement of the Hebrew laws.
There is one place only in the Koran where he makes mention of the
"tables" (alwāḥ = lūḥōth) given to Moses at Sinai, and the whole context there is very significant. He mentions the forty days spent by Moses
in the mount (Ex. 24:18), the seventy men afterward associated with
him (Num. 11:16, 24), and, three times over (vss. 142, 149, 153), the
heaven-sent tables containing "guidance and mercy for those who fear
their Lord." The emphasis on the episode of the golden calf (145–152),
like the subsequent catalogue of the sins of the Israelites (160–170), has
for its purpose the teaching, insisted upon by Mohammed in his own
lawgiving, that some of the statutes were given to the people because
of their unworthiness to receive better ones.[61] Moses asks (154), "Wilt
thou destroy us for what our foolish ones have done?" His Lord replies

---

[61] [Thus, for example, 4:158; and compare Mark 10:5, Matt. 19:8].

(155), "My chastisement shall fall on whom I will; but my mercy embraces all things, and I will write it down. . . . . (156) for those who shall follow the Apostle, the Prophet of the *goyim*, whom they shall find described in the Law and the Gospel. *He will enjoin upon them what is right, and forbid them what is wrong; he will make lawful for them the foods which are good, and prohibit for them those which are bad* (cf. 3:44, etc.); *and he will relieve them of their burden and the yokes which they have been carrying"*—a phrase which brings to mind the words of St. Paul. But Mohammed, unlike Paul, was legislating.

We may now consider the Koranic precepts in some detail, giving attention only to those which are either taken over directly from the Hebrew legislation or else appear to show its influence.

1. The Religious Legislation

This can be treated briefly, for the facts are well known, and have often been set forth. The "religion of Abraham," to which Mohammed so often appeals, was pure monotheism, in sharp opposition to idolatry. The first two commandments of the Hebrew Decalogue were foundation stones of Islam from the very first. Allah the one and only God; without image or likeness; destruction decreed upon all the idols and symbols of the pagans. The parallel between the Muslim *shahāda*, "There is no god but Allah," and the Hebrew Shema' is hardly accidental. That which is especially significant is not the content, nor the form, but the religious use. Mohammed certainly had some acquaintance with the Jewish ritual, and must have been profoundly impressed by the emphasis laid on the declaration of Deut. 6:4 f. It was not only the introduction to every formal service of prayer, and otherwise given very frequent repetition, but was also the Hebrew declaration of faith. "In reciting the first sentence of the Shema', a man takes upon him the yoke of the Kingdom of Heaven" (Moore, *Judaism*, I, 465, quoting Mishna *Ber.* 2, 2). This is precisely Mohammed's conception of the *shahāda* ("testimony"); see for example Sura 3:16, "God witnesses that there is no god but he; and the angels, and men who have knowledge, standing firm in the truth, declare, 'There is no god but he'!" Cf. also 13:29, and Jonah's saving declaration

(21:87), which rescued him from the whale's belly. There is to be added the Muslim *tauḥīd*, the confession of God's *unity*, as in Sura 112:1, and in the cry (also battle-cry) *aḥad, aḥad!* of the believers, which is very strikingly reminiscent of the mighty *eḥad!* which ends the first sentence of the Shemaʿ. All in all, it seems highly probable that Mohammed's *shahāda* was modeled directly upon the Hebrew formula.

As for the Decalogue as a whole, Mohammed does not give its laws any especial prominence. Each of the ten commandments has its counterpart in the Koran, however. He presumably (like many ancient and modern interpreters) thought of the third commandment as the prohibition of invoking the name of God in a false oath. See 2:224 f. and 5:91. The Jewish sabbath he had thrown overboard while he was in Mekka. The burden of one day in seven in which there could be no trading and no fighting was too heavy for his program. He chose to regard the sabbath law as one of those which were made severe for the sake of temporary discipline, saying in 16:124 f.,[62] "The sabbath was imposed only on those who were in disagreement concerning it; and verily thy Lord will judge between them, on the day of resurrection, concerning that about which they disagreed." For the Muslim day of prayer he selected the *ʿarūba* (Day of Preparation) of the Jews. Whether he knew that the Christians in his part of the world observed the first day of the week (if indeed they did) is not to be learned from the Koran.

The borrowing for the Mohammedan ritual was not merely from statute law; time-honored custom was also laid under contribution. The matter of the *qibla* (that is, the direction in which the worshipper turns his face in prayer) has already received mention. Mohammed began by directing his adherents to face Jerusalem in prayer (cf. Dan. 6:11, I Esdr. 4:58, Tobit 3:11 f., Judith 9:1); but when the Jews refused support, after the arrival in Medina, the order was changed in favor of the Kaʿba at Mekka. How keenly Mohammed felt the need of justifying this change, is shown by the length and the vehemence of his utterance in regard

---

[62] [In a former lecture I gave my reasons for thinking Nöldeke-Schwally mistaken in assigning these verses to the Medina period].

to it (2:136–146). He stood in awe of the Jews, and his argument is addressed (indirectly) to them, as well as to his own followers. "The foolish of the people will say, What has turned them from the *qibla* which they had? Say: The East and the West belong to Allah." He then explains that God gave them the former prescription merely as a test, to separate the believers from the unbelievers. Henceforth all Muslims must turn their faces "toward the sacred Mosque," wherever they may be (139, 144 f.). Gabriel assures the prophet that this is the true and final prescription, and that the Jews "recognize it as they recognize their own sons," but will not admit it. "No amount of signs and wonders would make them follow your *qibla,* and you are not to follow their *qibla*" (140 f.).

The regulations concerning prayer are very obviously derived in the main from Jewish usage. The facts relating to the latter are concisely stated, with full references, in Moore's *Judaism,* II, 216 f., 222. For the early Islamic usage see especially Mittwoch, *Zur Entstehungsgeschichte des islamischen Gebets und Cultus* (Abhandlungen der preuss. Akad., 1913). In both rituals the preliminary ablutions are indispensable (Sura 5:8, etc.). In both, the worshipper prays standing, and then with certain prescribed genuflections and prostrations. The attitudes of the orthodox Mohammedan prayer, which in their essential features undoubtedly represent the prophet's own practice, are best described and pictured in E. W. Lane's *Manners and Customs of the Modern Egyptians.* There is in the Koran no prescription of the *five* daily prayers, and it is not clear that they were instituted by Mohammed.[63] It is not like him to ordain a five-fold service even for *one* day in the week. What he commands in the

---

[63] [Goldziher, ZDMG. 53 (1899), p. 385; *Jewish Encycl.,* "Islam," p. 653; suggested that the five daily prayers were instituted under the influence of the five prayer times of the Persians. This seems hardly probable. Simon Duran, in his *Qesheth u-Magen* (c. 1400), ed. Steinschneider, 1881, p. 14, asserted that the Muslims borrowed the custom from the Jews, because "there are five prayers on the Yom ha-Kippurim." Joseph Sambari, in his Chronicle (17th century), Bodleian MS., fol. 7, repeats this from Duran. (I owe these latter references to my former pupil, Dr. Philip Grossman, who is preparing the Chronicle for publication.) It seems more likely that the wish to surpass the Jews in devotion, and at the same time to compensate for an inconvenient nocturnal *ṣalāt al-wusṭā* (see below), produced this series of prayer seasons, soon after the death of the prophet].

Koran is characteristic. It is simple, reasonable, and like other features of
the new legislation in its adaptation of an already existing ritual to
Arabian conditions. The traditional Jewish prescription was three daily
prayers, as e. g. in Dan. 6:11. In four passages (11:116, 17:80 f., 50:38 f.,
76:25 f.), all from the Mekka period, the prophet directs his followers to
pray three times in the day: in the morning, at eventide, and *in the night*
—a time better suited to the Bedouin traveling under the stars than to
the city-dweller.[64] Not that prayer is in any way limited to these seasons.
Like the Jewish legislators, the prophet reiterates that a man must pray
often, whenever and wherever he feels the need; then letting nothing
interfere with his devotions or take his thought from them. Prayer may
be curtailed in time of danger, 4:102; cf. the Mishna *Ber.* iv, 4. In verse
104 (this being a Sura of the Medina period) it is said that the times of
prayer have already been prescribed. The prayer must not be uttered in
a loud voice, nor in a whisper, 17:110; so also *Erub.* 64 a and *Ber.* 31 a. The
drunken man may not pray, 4:46; so *Ber., ibid.* The correspondence of
the Koran with the Rabbinical precepts is noticeable throughout.

"Grace before meat" was always insisted upon in the Jewish laws. It
had been customary in pagan Arabia to pronounce the *tahlil* over
slaughtered beasts, and Mohammed takes account of this fact in his legislation; but it is quite evident that what he intended to prescribe for his
adherents was an approximation to the Jewish custom. "Eat of the lawful
and good food which Allah has provided for you, and thank the bounty
of your Lord," 16:115; also 2:167, 5:6, 6:118 ff., 22:35 ff. The Mohammedan
of modern times must at least say *Bismillah* ("In the name of God") before
partaking of food; Lane, *Manners and Customs*, I, 183. For the earliest
period, a few lines from a little poem composed but a short time after the
death of the prophet may serve for illustration. A notorious jailbird who
had flown to a cave in the mountains, and for some time lived there in
fierce partnership with a leopard, reproaches the beast for being no
Muslim: [65]

---

[64] [Is it not altogether probable (in spite of the commentators) that the "*ṣalāt al-wusṭā*"
of 2:239 intends this nocturnal prayer?].

[65] [Nöldeke, *Delectus Vet. Carm. Arab.*, p. 50].

In the steep mountain side a cave was waiting;
   I share its shelter with a new-found friend,
Old Brownie, noble partner, fitting comrade—
   Were he but better able to unbend!

Our conversation, when we meet, is silence,
   And darting glances, sharp as any blade.
Each were a foe, saw he one sign of shrinking;
   But like met like, and generous terms we made.

Down in the rocks a water hole is hidden,
   Where we must needs resort to quench our thirst.
Each in his turn, we near the spot with caution,
   And give full time to him who gains it first.

The mountain goats afford us choice provision,
   We share alike the booty of the chase.
I, true believer, eat mine with a blessing,
   But he, ungodly wretch, will say no grace!

The primitive Mohammedan service of the "mosque" (*masgid* is an old Aramaic word, common in the Nabataean inscriptions), consisting of prayer, reading from the Koran, and an address, was prescribed by the existing conditions; and yet presumably in the main (like the weekly day of worship) suggested to Mohammed by the service of the synagogue. That at any rate was close at hand and well known to him. After his time, the service was given a more elaborate form, apparently patterned on that of the Christians; see Becker in *Islam*, 3, 384. As soon as the Muslim world found its chief centers in Syria, Egypt, and Mesopotamia, the Christian praxis became very influential; but in the earlier time there is no feature of either ritual or terminology, in the mosque service, that can with any probability be attached to Christian usage.[66]

66 [Brockelmann, in the Sachau *Festschrift*, 314–320, argues acutely for the Christian origin of the technical term for the initiation of the prayer-service, *iqāmat aṣ-ṣalāt*, deriving

The fast of the month Ramaḍān (2:181 ff.) has already been mentioned as probably suggested to Mohammed by the Christian lenten season. It may be doubted whether he had any definite knowledge as to the manner in which the Christian fast was kept. The Jewish customs of fasting were of course known to him. The *manner* of fasting, abstaining altogether during the day, and eating and drinking after sundown, was Jewish. Another of the many proofs of Mohammed's truly extensive acquaintance with the Jewish ordinances is to be seen in 2:183, where the beginning of the new day (in the month of fasting) is defined as the time "when a white thread can be distinguished from a black thread"; a mode of determining which certainly is taken over directly from the rabbinical prescription in the Mishna (*Ber.* I, 2), where it has reference to the uttering of the Shema'. The provision for the man who is ill or on a journey, permitting him to keep the fast at another time (2:180 f.), resembles the prescription of the "little passover" in Num. 9:9-11. The oft-repeated and apparently strongly supported tradition, according to which Mohammed at first ordered his followers to fast, like the Jews, on the Day of Atonement, but later substituted Ramaḍān, has been accepted as genuine by many modern scholars (Geiger, 36 f., Nöldeke-Schwally, I, 179, Margoliouth, *Mohammed,* 250), but is of very doubtful validity. The subject of the prophet's break with the Jews was so interesting that it called forth numerous "traditions" of the sort (see Margoliouth, *ibid.*). If by his authority the month had been substituted for the day, the latter would certainly have been dropped altogether by the Muslims. The fast of the tenth of Moharram (Lane, *Manners and Customs,* II, 148 f.) must have arisen—like so much else!—after the time of Moham-

it from the Syriac terminology. It is a tangled problem, for the verb in question has very wide and varied use in both languages, and the development in the one is almost always paralleled in the other. The fact of borrowing seems to be established by Brockelmann; but this conclusion does not touch the earliest Muslim usage, which is, and should be kept, quite distinct. Whatever adoption of the Christian formula there was, must have taken place in the time of the Omayyads. In the Koran, Moh. uses the verb *qūm* as the technical term, "pray," in several passages: see 2:239, 4:103, 9:85, 109 (twice); and cf. 18:13. The term probably had its origin simply in the worshipper's attitude (see above), and it is significant that in the Jewish terminology *'amīda* was thus used (Mittwoch, *op. cit.;* cf. Geiger, 84 f.). The varied Koranic use of *aqāma* is in every case most naturally explained as purely native Arabic.]

med. The name, 'āshūrā,' is Aramaic, and the fast coincided, exactly or nearly, with the Jewish fast; but this is all that can be said with certainty.

The Pilgrimage to Mekka hardly requires mention, for it was a long-established Arabian custom; its adoption important to Mohammed not only for the sake of its appeal to the tribes, but also for the solidarity of Islam. It may be conjectured, however, that its incorporation in the Muslim ritual was also recommended to the prophet by the familiar picture of Jerusalem as the center of the world, the city toward which all exiles and pilgrims turn their faces.

2. The Social Legislation [67]

In the social laws of the Koran, in the regulations touching the family, the Muslim community, business transactions, and the punishment of crime, the influence of Jewish legislation, both earlier and later, appears very distinctly.

The duty of the child, and of the man in mature age, to revere his parents and to care for them, was a cardinal principle of Arabian family life long before Mohammed's time. The poems and tales of the nomadic tribes give abundant illustration. The head of the family was honored and obeyed, and the mother had her minor share of respect. Here again, however, Mohammed turns to the Hebrew decalogue for new authority. In several Suras of the Mekkan period he speaks of an ordinance long ago given by God to men. In 17:24 we read: "Your Lord ordained that you should serve no other god but him; and that you should do good to your father and mother, whether one or both of them attain to old age with you." In 31:13 and 46:14 likewise, the divine commandment is said to have been given "to mankind." It might seem superfluous to look for influence of previous legislation in regard to a duty so universally recognized as that of children to their parents. But Mohammed cannot have been ignorant of the fact that this one of the Ten Commandments was given especial weight by the Jews; and he must have been interested to know how the "people of the Book" interpreted the ordinance. It is ob-

---

[67] [This subject is very well treated by R. Roberts, *The Social Laws of the Qorān* (London, 1925), who takes account also of the Jewish practice].

vious that with the command of monotheism heading the list, both in position and in importance, the only one of the remaining nine which could naturally be given the second place is the Fifth. This fact may sufficiently account for Mohammed's collocation of the two commandments (in 17:24); but it is more likely that he had been impressed by the ancient and oft-repeated rabbinic teaching. In both Talmud and oldest midrashim, "Honor thy father and mother" and "Honor the Lord" are expressly yoked together.

In other phases of the same subject the Koran and Jewish teaching are in an agreement which can hardly be altogether accidental. In Lev. 19:3 reverence for the mother is placed before that for the father; the order being doubtless intentional, as teaching the equality of the two parents in this regard. Here is the atmosphere of Palestine rather than of Arabia; but in two of the Koranic passages just cited (31:13; 46:14) the claim of the mother is the one dwelt upon, with mention of the discomfort of pregnancy, the pain of childbirth, the "thirty months" of nursing, and the subsequent care. The old Hebrew laws visited severe punishment on the disobedient son. In the Mohammedan legislation disobedience to parents (*'uqūqu 'l-wālidaini*) is one of the seven "great" sins (see Beiḍāwī's comment on Sura 4:35). On the other hand, the Talmud, *Yebamoth* 5 b, 6 a, expressly declares that a son must not obey a paternal command which is contrary to the divine ordinances. Thus also the Koran: 29:7, 'If your parents should urge you to join to my worship that of other gods, do not obey them, it is to me that you have to give account.' The same command is given in 31:14.

In general, the injunctions so often laid upon the son or daughter in the rabbinical writings are those which we find in the Koran. 'Speak kindly to your parents, submit to their will, and show your affection for them' (17:24 f.). The prophet Noah, when the deluge is about to begin, manifests his filial piety by praying for his parents (71:29); though the event shows that they were such old reprobates as to make his petition unavailing.

A cardinal Mohammedan duty, one of the five "pillars of Islam," is the giving of alms. No other practical duty is so constantly reiterated by the prophet throughout the Koran. This is indeed an obligation recognized in every civilized and half-civilized community. The poor, the helpless, the unfortunate, must be cared for. Generosity was a characteristic virtue of the pre-Mohammedan Arabs. The two technical terms, however, adopted by the prophet for the exercise of Muslim charity are both borrowed from the North-Semitic vocabulary, and therefore doubtless point to North-Semitic practice. The Koranic term zakāt, "righteousness" (originally "purity") is the Aramaic זָכוּת, employed in this general sense, "virtuous conduct" and the like, by both Jews and Christians. The other term, ṣadaqa(t), is the Aramaic צִדְקְתָא, Hebrew צְדָקָה having the same meaning. We know that the latter term was widely used in Aramaic speech to mean "alms." It is used thus in the Koran, especially in the latest Suras, but only occasionally and somewhat indefinitely.[68] As for zakāt, the word constantly employed in all parts of the Koran, we have no direct evidence that its Aramaic prototype was ever used to mean "alms," among either Jews or Christians, prior to the spread of Islam in Western Asia. It may be that Mohammed himself originated in the case of this word the easy transition, "righteousness, meritorious action, almsgiving," which had long ago taken place in the use of the other word. Far more probably, however, zakāt had been given the meaning "alms" in the speech of the Arabian Jews—in regard to which we have very little knowledge. At the outset of Mohammed's public teaching we see him employing derivatives of the root zakā in a theological terminology which unquestionably is of Jewish origin (see 80:3, 7; 87:14; 91:9; 92:18).

The great emphasis laid upon almsgiving by the Jewish teachers, from Daniel (4:24) and the book of Tobit (4:7–11, 16 f.) onward, is faithfully reproduced in the Koran and the Muslim tradition. Sura 3:85 f: 'Those who die in unbelief are not ransomed from hell by any amount of charity, even though they have given the earth full of gold.' And then, addressing the true believers: "You cannot attain to righteousness unless

---

[68] [In 58:14 there is a clear distinction between the zakāt, which is definitely prescribed, and the ṣadaqa, which is not. On both terms see especially Snouck Hurgronje in the *Revue de l'histoire des Religions*, vol. 30 (1894), 163–167; Nöldeke, *Neue Beiträge zur semitischen Sprachwissenschaft*, 25].

you expend of that which you love; and whatever you expend, God knows
it." Thus also 57:7-12, and many other passages. Koran and *ḥadīth* repeat
the Jewish doctrine, that almsgiving atones for sin. Rabbi Judah is quoted
in *Baba Bathra* 10 a as saying, "So great is almsgiving that it brings re-
demption near." With this may be compared a saying of 'Omar ibn
'Abd al-'Azīz: [69] "Prayer carries us half-way to God; fasting brings us to
the door of his palace; and almsgiving procures for us admission." In
such an interesting collection of moral and religious tales as the *Ḥibbūr
Yaphē* of Rabbi Nissīm ben Jacob (11th century), the original Arabic
of which is now being published by Professor Obermann, the reiteration
of this teaching, that deeds of charity insure a place in the *'ōlām habbā,*
is very noticeable. This is also true of the Mohammedan religious narratives, early and late.

It was always a fundamental principle of the Hebrew-Jewish teaching
in regard to the bestowal of charity that the kindly feeling of the giver
is of greater value than the gift (Moore, *Judaism,* II, 171 f.). Mohammed
can hardly have failed to hear this doctrine, and it may be that we hear
a conscious echo of it in Sura 2:265 f.: "Kindly speech and pardon of
injury are better than charity followed by unkind treatment. . . . . O
you who believe, make not your almsgiving ineffectual by uttering reproaches, or by conduct that gives vexation." There are one or two early
passages in the Koran, dealing with charity in general, that sound like a
reminiscence of Old Testament prophecy, a bit out of Second Isaiah. In
Sura 90:11 ff. the impious and selfish rich man is assailed. "He does not
attempt the steep path. And how dost thou know what the steep path
is? It is setting free the captives; giving food in the day of famine; to
the orphan, him who is near of kin; or to the poor man who lies in the
dust. It is to be of those who believe, who encourage one another to patience and to deeds of mercy." A similar utterance is 76:8.

Contributions for the support of the poor and helpless in Islam were
at first voluntary, later compulsory. While the Muslims were in Mekka
there was no need of a "community chest." Mohammed's exhortations to
charity were for the benefit of the giver rather than of the receiver; they

---

[69] [Quoted in Roberts, *Social Laws of the Qorān,* p. 74].

had in view the comforts of the next world, rather than of the present. After the flight to Yathrib the conditions were very different. Contributions to a Muslim fund were indispensable from the first, and the need became more and more urgent. Not only the care of the poor, but the support of an increasing multitude of undertakings, peaceful and warlike, called for constant donations from all who were able to give. The Koran urges this duty with great and ever-increasing emphasis. A definite portion of certain gains made by the Muslims, such as the booty taken in warfare, was set aside for the common fund (8:42, and elsewhere): "Whatever booty you gain, the fifth part belongs to Allah and his prophet"; and the probable use of it is specified as aid to "kindred and orphans and the poor and the wayfarer." The origin of his prescription of "the fifth" is obscure. Professor Ginzberg has suggested to me the possibility of its derivation from the rabbinical ordinance which sets one-fifth as the maximum for charity. Thus *Kethuboth* 50 a, "He who will spend (his property in charity) must not spend more than the fifth part"; that is, he must not squander his goods even for a worthy end. Similarly Jer. *Peah* 15 a, "It was the saying at Usha that a man may spend one-fifth of his property in almsgiving." This might perhaps have suggested to Mohammed the fraction which he adopts in his law. Another possibility has occurred to me, in consideration of the fact that the Koranic regulation is not concerned with individuals, but with wealth acquired by the state. The first Muslim to legislate concerning state property was the prophet Joseph, who instituted a communistic régime in Egypt, and designated a fifth part of the produce of the land for its ruler: "And Joseph made it a statute concerning the land of Egypt unto this day, that Pharaoh should have the fifth" (Gen. 47:24–26). This certainly was well known to Mohammed; and it is at least an interesting parallel, that one-fifth of the wealth acquired by the Muslim state was to be turned over "to Allah and his prophet," to be administered as the latter saw fit. The ideas of Mohammed and his companions as to the proportion of a man's property which he might be expected to contribute "in the way of God" are nowhere in the Koran reflected more definitely than in the general prescription, that each must give "all that he can spare" (2:217 f.). Very soon after the prophet's death, however, the *zakāt* was made a definite tax, to be exacted from all Muslims.

In all this we may see combined the working of practical necessity; the duty of giving to God, recognized in every religion and in all parts of the world; and the undoubted influence of Jewish, and perhaps also Christian, enactments and customs. In particular, the Hebrew-Jewish law of tithes, which certainly was known to Mohammed, must have given suggestions to him, as well as to the lawgivers who followed him.

The law of retaliation, "an eye for an eye and a tooth for a tooth," was obeyed in many parts of the ancient world. It is especially familiar in the early Semitic legislation, beginning with the Hammurabi Code and the Mosiac Law. In the history of the pre-Mohammedan Arabs, blood-revenge plays a very conspicuous part, as is well known. The Koran expressly appeals to the authority of the Hebrew scriptures in its legislation concerning these matters. In Sura 5:48 the Hebrew Torah is said to be a source of light and guidance; and verse 49 proceeds: "We prescribed for them in it that life should pay for life, eye for eye, nose for nose, ear for ear, tooth for tooth, and for wounds retaliation (Ex. 21:23, 25); but if any one shall remit it as alms, this shall make atonement for the crime." The word *Kaffāra,* "atonement," cannot fail to recall the כֹּפֶר of Ex. 21:30, which in *Mechilta* (on 21:24) is expressly applied by Rabbi Isaac to the minor injuries here named, and is constantly used in the Talmud where these matters are dealt with. Certainly an Arabic term coined by the Jews of the Hijaz. Mohammed follows both the rabbinical authorities and old Arab custom in permitting payment instead of retaliation; but when this mode of restitution is made to include cases of deliberate murder, he agrees with his ancestors but not with the Old Testament. So also the special law concerning the killing of one Muslim by another (4:94) has no resemblance to Israelite legislation, but is based primarily on Arabian custom. The tendency of the Rabbis was always toward a milder interpretation of the law; there is no better illustration of the fact than the extended comment in *Mechilta* on these verses in Ex. 21. They knew that retaliation is likely to keep the door of revenge open rather than to close it. As Rabbi Dosethai ben Judah remarks, in *Baba Qamma*

83 b, "If the eye of the injured party is a large one, and the eye destroyed in exchange for it is a small one, is the matter settled?" The Arabs were a hot-blooded people. In the processes of blood-revenge which brought on the celebrated War of Basūs, al-Ḥārith ibn 'Ubād demands: "Did you kill the youth Bujair in payment for Kulaib? Is the affair then settled?" The contemptuous answer is given: "I killed him for a shoestring of Kulaib!" "That," retorted al-Ḥārith, "is putting the price of shoestrings too high"; and the war was on.[70] Mohammed has something of this sort in mind when he says (Sura 22:59), "Whoever punishes with an injury like that which has been inflicted on him, and then is outraged again, God will surely help him." How this divine aid will be given, is not specified; probably the working principle would be, that God helps those who help themselves.

Mohammed, while ruthless in dealing with his foes, was mild by nature. He not only allows payment, in camels, or sheep, or what not, for every sort of injury, including murder; but also repeatedly advises his followers to forgive, instead of exacting the full penalty. The law of retaliation stood, nevertheless. Not long after the migration to Medina, two young women of the Muslims engaged in a quarrel which began with words and ended with blows. One of the two, ar-Rubayyiʿ bint an-Naḍr, member of an influential family, succeeded in knocking out one of the front teeth of her opponent. The family of the latter demanded vengeance according to the ancient law. It was a clear case, and Mohammed pronounced accordingly. But Anas, the brother of the culprit, arose in his wrath and swore to Mohammed, 'by Him who had sent him as a prophet,' that his sister's front tooth should *not* be broken out. Now Anas was a mighty Muslim—he fell, somewhat later, in the battle of Ohod, after performing prodigies of valor—and his protest, reinforced by the oath, held up the execution of the sentence. Mohammed finally prevailed on the injured family to accept payment instead of retaliation (Bokhari, ed. Krehl, II, 203 f.).

When the Koran comes to deal with regulations concerning trade and the transaction of business, we might expect to find very little evidence of

[70] [*Ḥamāsa*, ed. Freytag, 251 f.]

influence from Jewish legislation. The city Arabs were traders of long experience. Mohammed himself had been a merchant. Aside from the local caravans and the through traffic threading the Hijaz, there were especially the four sacred months of the pagan Arabs and the great annual fair at 'Ukāẓ; portions of the year largely given over to peaceful trading among the tribes. The basal rules of commerce were of long standing, and hardly to be altered even by a prophet. There were nevertheless matters of importance, not regulated by any general Arabian law, concerning which some prescription was necessary or desirable. How should debtors be treated? Should the Muslim exact interest when making a loan to his fellow-Muslim? May a man pursue his trade on Friday as freely as on other days? Questions similar to these, and to still others with which the Koran deals, had been answered by the Hebrew lawgivers and interpreters; and it is from their decisions especially that Mohammed derives his own doctrine.

The general principles of fair dealing in bargains and commerce could be taken for granted. This subject was touched upon in a preceding lecture. No man in Arabia would have questioned, in theory, the rule that the same weights should be used in selling as in buying; or that an article of merchandise ought to be what its owner declares it to be. In practice, there were other maxims—as in other lands. *Caveat emptor;* "the buyer has need of a hundred eyes, the seller has need of but one." The Muslim community had especial need of definite rules. Mohammed saw the desirability of written contracts; and the Koran requires at least two witnesses to formal business documents, as well as in criminal cases (Sura 2:282). In ordinary bargains and loans no writing is required (2:283 f.); it is taken for granted that a man will stand by his word—as in the Jewish practice.

How to deal with the delinquent debtor, was not an easy question. The debtor is quite likely to regard himself as the injured party, if payment is requested, and to resent any attempt to collect the amount which is due. The creditor is always in the wrong. The way in which many of the Arabs were inclined to look at this matter can be seen in a series of poems collected in Buḥturī's *Ḥamāsa,* in each of which the joy of the debtor's triumph over his pursuer is shared by his friends. One of the delinquents, a Bedouin whose creditor was a merchant of Medina, tells how the latter, armed with the promissory paper and accompanied by several companions, caught him at last in the city. He managed to slip out of their hands, and ran "at a speed no bird could equal." He heard one of them say: "No use; impossible to catch him; let the Bedouins go to hell." He shouted back: "Payment postponed! Fold up the paper, and keep the mice away from it." (*Ḥamāsa,* ed. Cheikho, pp. 263 f.) Another sings complacently (*ibid.,* 261, bottom):

> He counted, on the fingers of his hands,
>> The dinars which he fondly thought to gain.
> Better might he have tried to count the years
>> That must elapse while he pursues in vain.
> He looks for usury; ah, lucky man,
>> If e'er he sees his principal again!

Still another describes with enthusiasm the preparation which he has made for the expected visit of his creditors (*ibid.,* 263): "I have ready an excellent cudgel of *arzan* wood, thick, strong, with projecting knots."

These verses, and others like them, were recited, handed about, and preserved in anthologies, chiefly because of the popular sympathy with this "under dog," the poor debtor. If the creditor had a surplus which he could lend (with or without interest), is it not evident that he could get along without it? Hebrew and Arabian lawgivers felt this pressure. The warm-hearted legislation of Deuteronomy would cancel all debts in the seventh year. (Deut. 15:1 f.). Mohammed was naturally unable to make any use of this law for his Arabian commonwealth; but where he introduces the subject of debts in the Koran (2:280) a sabbatical year seems hardly necessary. He says: "If the debtor is in straitened circumstances, let the matter wait until easier times; but if you remit the debt as alms, it is better for you." The actual Mohammedan legal practice, however, almost from the first, corresponded to the ancient Hebrew usage. The debtor may be imprisoned (cf. Matt. 5:25); he may be compelled to do work in discharge of the debt—the usual recourse where the delinquent is able-bodied; but in no case could free-born Hebrew or Muslim be reduced by his fellows to the status of a mere slave.

In regard to usury, also, the old Hebrew enactments are repeated in the Koran. The Muslim must not exact interest from his fellow-believer, but there is no such restriction when he is dealing with non-Muslims (cf. 2:276–279 with Ex. 22:25 and Deut. 23:19). As in the Jewish usage, the law is concerned not merely with loans of money, but with all bartering or other business transaction in which one seeks profit by another's loss. If the Hebrew takes interest from his brother, Deut. 23:20 declares that God will not prosper his business; and in Sura 30:38 we read: "Whatever you put out at interest, to gain increase from the property of others, will have no increase from God." If debts are witnessed, there must be no bribery of witnesses or judges (2:282; 2:184).

In regard to business transactions on Friday, Mohammed of course legislates for people who were primarily traders rather than tillers of the soil. He could have no use for anything like the strict Jewish law of the sabbath; his prescription would more nearly resemble the looser practice of the Christians. He only insists that trading must cease during the Friday service in the mosque; and he refers with some bitterness to his own unpleasant experience on the occasion when his audience deserted him, because of the arrival of a caravan at Medina, when he was in the midst of a sermon. And it would seem that something of the sort had happened more than once. Gabriel says to Mohammed (62:11), "When they saw an opportunity of trade, or some diversion, they flocked out to it and left you standing. Say to them: That which is with God is better than any diversion or trading!" The view has often been expressed, by the more devout Mohammedan teachers, that the whole day Friday should be kept free from worldly business, and devoted to the business of the life to come.

In the early Mohammedan laws relating to marriage and divorce, concubines, adultery, and the various family relations, there is comparatively little evidence of Jewish influence. The chief determining factors were old Arabian practice, obvious requirement, and Mohammed's own rather strong leanings.

Sura 4:26 f. gives a list of the near relatives with whom marriage is not permitted; and in 24:31 are enumerated those members of the household in whose presence women may be unveiled, or even unclad. Comparison of these lists with those in Lev. 18:6–18 and 20:11–21 shows almost perfect agreement. Mohammed indeed prohibits marriage with a niece, which in the Old Testament is permitted. It here seems plain that he was acquainted with the Hebrew laws (Roberts, *Social Laws of the Qorān*, p. 14). The Muslims are permitted to marry Jewish and Christian women, but not the pagan Arabs. As to marriage with slaves, the law is substantially that of Deut. 20:10–14.

The very unsatisfactory legislation of Islam regarding divorce has little resemblance to the Jewish ordinances. The general statement as to the ground of divorce, namely the man's dissatisfaction with his wife (e. g. Sura 2, 226 f.), is not unlike that in Deut. 24:1; and in the Koran, as in the Jewish law, the right of divorce was given only to the husband. It is nevertheless hardly to be claimed that Mohammed and his followers were here guided by the Hebrew-Jewish enactments. There are on the other hand two definite prescriptions in the Koran which certainly were derived from the Talmud. The period of waiting in the case of a divorced wife is three months (Sura 2:228; cf. the Mishna, *Yebamoth* iv, 10); and the prescribed time for a woman to give suck to her child is two full years (Sura 2:233; cf. *Kethuboth* 60 a.)

Adultery was severely dealt with, as generally in the ancient world. The punishment prescribed in the Koran is flogging; doubtless the most natural form of punishment, and yet possibly suggested to Mohammed by the rabbinic law. The Mishna, *Kerithuth* ii, 4, prescribes forty stripes for the convicted female slave; and the Koran (4:30) raises the number to *fifty*, while the penalty for free men and women is twice the latter amount (24:2). There is to be noticed also the much-discussed verse which in the judgment of the best scholars, ancient and modern, once stood in the Koran, but was afterwards removed, as either abrogated or else not belonging to the original text (i. e. of Sura 33; see Nöldeke-Schwally, *Geschichte des Qorans,* pp. 248 ff.). The verse reads: "If a man and a woman, both of full age, commit the crime, stone them relentlessly; the punishment ordained of God." This sounds like Mohammed, and indeed the only reasonable supposition is that he himself composed it. Just when and where, however, did God ordain the penalty of stoning for this crime? In the New Testament, John 8:3–5, the scribes and Pharisees are quoted as saying to Jesus: "This woman has been taken in adultery. Now in the law Moses commanded us to stone such; what then sayest thou?" The Mosaic law known to us does not contain the ordinance, however. Has a verse been removed from the Pentateuch as well as from the Koran? Nor is this all. The passage in John containing the episode of the woman has been removed from the Gospel, as not having formed part of the original text. A strange fate seems to have pursued this particular statute! [71]

As to the status of children in the family and in the Muslim community there is a general resemblance, as would be expected, between the prescriptions of the Koran and the Israelite codes. We may see here the moral influence of the practice in the Jewish communities of Mekka and Medina, rather than imitation of specific enactments. The emphasis placed by Mohammed, from the very first, on the care of the orphan, is fully as strong as in the Old Testament. He also gives to the daughters of the family, as well as to the other female members, a status such as his countrymen had never given them. In the usage of the pagan Arabs the inferiority of daughters to sons was much more pronounced than it was among their Jewish neighbors. Mohammed put a stop to the barbarous practice of doing away with undesired female infants by burying them alive; he also gave to the Muslim women an altogether new standing through his legislation.

The laws of inheritance in the Koran are especially noteworthy in this regard. The custom of the pagan Arabs had excluded the daughter,

[71] [The difficulties are by no means insurmountable, however. Mohammed (if the words are really his) was thinking of the *mode* of punishment rather than of the particular crime; and in the Johannine passage the difficulty may be overcome by supposing a betrothed woman (Deut. 22:24)].

the widow, and every other female relative from any right to the family property. In the Hebrew law, on the contrary, there is the incident of the daughters of Zelophehad, Num. 27:1 ff., and the resulting legislation in vss. 8–11, specifying the successive heirs of one who ·dies leaving no son. It is noteworthy that the order of succession given in the Koran is the same as in the Hebrew law. Mohammed, however, goes still further in permitting the female relatives to benefit, as may be seen in Sura 4:12–15, and again, vs. 175. The sons and daughters of a female slave, if they have been acknowledged by the father of the family, may inherit in like manner.

The Hebrew and Mohammedan laws in regard to slavery resemble each other in many particulars. The Semites, as a race, have always shown the inclination to treat slaves leniently; as their legislation, from the Code of Hammurabi onward, bears witness. It must be borne in mind that with the Mohammedans, even more than with the Hebrews, the slave's religion was an important factor in determining his treatment. In the old Hebrew community, the slave who had accepted circumcision, even though not a proselyte, was a sharer in certain religious privileges, and was accordingly not on the same footing as one who had refused the rite—and who therefore, according to the rabbinical law, must be sold to a Gentile master after the expiration of a certain time. In the Mohammedan house, the slave was very likely to be a Muslim, and must be treated as such. There was never lack of harsh and even barbarous treatment, it is needless to say; and much of it, doubtless, was richly deserved; but we certainly have reason to believe that undue severity was the exception, not the rule, in both the Israelite and the Muslim community.

There remains one class of laws to be noticed briefly, namely those dealing with food and drink. In the legislation concerning food, Mohammed shows great interest in the Jewish laws, and evidently intends in a general way to imitate them. Conditions and customs in Arabia necessitated some differences, however. The laws of Israel are now superseded by the Muslim enactments: "The food of the people of the Book is lawful for you, and yours for them" (5:7). In 6:147 he specifies some of the Jewish prohibitions: "To those who were Jews we forbade everything that has a solid hoof; and of cattle and sheep we prohibited the fat, save that which is in their backs or their entrails, or attached to the bone." He insists, however, both here and in other passages, that these prohibitions were not *originally* given, but were of the nature of a punishment. Thus 4:158, "Because of the wrongdoing of the Jews we forbade them things which we had made lawful for them." 3:87, "All food was lawful to the children of Israel, except what Israel made unlawful to himself before the Law was revealed." In 2:167 f., 6:146, and 16:116, Mohammed enumerates things forbidden to Muslims: flesh of what is found dead, blood, swine's flesh, food offered to idols. 5:4 adds to this list: "What has been strangled, killed by a blow or a fall, or by goring; that of which wild beasts have eaten; and whatever has been slaughtered on heathen altars." [72] In 2:168, 5:5, and 16:116 Mohammed characteristically makes the exception, that if a man is forced to eat some one of these things, driven by his sore need of food, it is no sin. The Talmud, as is well known, says the same.

The Mohammedan prohibition of *wine-drinking* (which really means, the drinking of any intoxicating beverage) has an interesting history. The ancient Hebrews looked upon drunkenness as one of the serious evils. The story of Noah is an early illustration. One of the later writers says, "Wine is a mocker, strong drink is raging," and there are other similar utterances. The Hebrew ideal, however, was always temperance, by the man's exercise of self-control. "Wine that maketh glad the heart of man" is classed as a blessing, and has a very honorable place in the scriptures. Such a saint as Rabbi Meïr (if the popular tales can be credited) might become intoxicated, under suitable circumstances, without damage to his reputation. [73]

The legislation of the Koran in regard to strong drink shows a change of attitude. At the outset Mohammed held the liberal view represented by the Hebrew scriptures and the subsequent Jewish custom. In Sura 16:67–71 the prophet gives a list of the special blessings freely given by

---

[72] [The most of these prohibitions were all but universal in the ancient civilized world. See also Mishna *Chullin*, 3, Bab. *Chullin*, 39 ff.].

[73] [See *The Arabic Original of the Ḥibbūr Yaphē*, ed. Obermann, pp. 121–123].

God to men, enumerating four: water, milk, *wine,* and honey. Sura
47:16 assures the true believers that they shall have plenty of wine in
paradise. But in 2:216 and 5:92 f. this approval begins to be qualified. How
the change came about, what reflection or what happenings may have
influenced him, it probably is useless to conjecture. Even here, in the
latter years of his career, the prohibition is at first quite mild. 2:216: "They
will ask you about wine, and *al-maisir"* (a form of gambling). "Say:
In them both is sin [74] and profit to men; but the sin of both is greater
than the profit." 4:46 suggests a religious community in which prohibition,
if really existing, was recognized as imperfectly effective: "O you believers!
Come not to prayer when you are drunk, until you know what you are
saying." This injunction may have had its origin in the prophet's experience, or (like so many other prescriptions regarding prayer) have been
taken over from the Mishnic law, *Ber.* 31 a. The passage 5:92 f., in one
of the very latest Suras, has a much more decided sound: "O you who
believe! Verily wine, and *al-maisir* . . . . are an abomination, of Satan's
work; avoid them then, that haply you may prosper. Satan desires to put
enemity and hatred among you by wine and *al-maisir,* and to turn you
away from the remembrance of God, and from prayer."

After the prophet's death, the prohibition was sharpened in Muslim law,
perhaps especially under the rule of the stern and ascetic caliph Omar.
There is nothing in the possible influence of non-Muslim communities
or practices to account for this. As far as Christian usage is concerned, we
know that some of the Arabs who preferred Christianity to Islam were
taunted with making the choice because within that fold they could enjoy
their intoxicating drink unmolested. Early traditions begin to put a very
strong emphasis on the law forbidding wine. An old Egyptian *ḥadīth* puts
into the mouth of the prophet a list of prohibitions which bears considerable resemblance to certain modern enactments. A solemn curse is pronounced on any one "who drinks wine, or gives it to drink; sells it, or
buys it; carries it, or has it brought to him; presses it out, or has another

[74] [Our Koran text says, *"great* sin," but the objection to the adjective *ḳebīr,* on stylistic
grounds, is well taken (Nöldeke-Schwally, 182, note 3). The word was added later, hardly
by the prophet himself].

press it out for him; takes possession of it, or profits from its price" (Ibn 'Abd al-Hakam's *Futūḥ Miṣr*, 264 f.). Another tradition of the same early period makes Mohammed declare that wine-drinking is "the chief of all sins"! (*ibid.*, 271). It is plain that popular resistance to the increasing rigor of the law was the cause of this exaggeration.

Still another outwardly authentic *ḥadīth*, also of Egyptian origin, provides an illustrative ancedote. A man named Dailam, of the tribe of Jaishān, narrates as follows (*ibid.*, 303). "I came to the prophet, and said to him, O Prophet of God, we live in a region where it is very cold in winter, and we make a strong drink from grain; is that permitted? He said, Does it not intoxicate? I answered, Surely! Then it is forbidden, he said. But I came to him a second time, with the same question; and he gave the same answer. I returned, however, once more, and said: See now, O Prophet of God; how, if they refuse to give it up, because the habit has got possession of them? He answered, Whenever you find a man who is overcome by the habit, kill him!"

The history of this law is like that of not a few others in Islam. New circumstances and needs wrought changes. The varied influence of Judaism (and also, perhaps even more strikingly, of Christianity) continued to be potent in the generations subsequent to the death of the prophet. The laws and customs of the "people of the Book" did not cease to make their profound impression; and considerable portions of the Jewish haggada, in particular, were taken over into the Muslim literature and carried back, in pseudo-tradition, to the Companions, or to the prophet himself. The orthodox tradition itself grew up under the influence of the Jewish tradition. All this is of very minor importance, however, in comparison with the undeniable fact, that the very foundations of Mohammedanism were laid deep in an Arabian Judaism which was both learned and authoritative, altogether worthy of its Palestinian and Babylonian ancestry.

INDEXES

I. Names and Subjects

II. Arabic names and words discussed

a. NAMES

b. WORDS

III. Passages Cited

a. The Koran

b. The Scriptures

c. Talmud and Midrash